DEC. 2011

Test Results for Digital Data Acquisition Tool:
Tableau TD1 Forensic Duplicator; Firmware
Version 2.34 Feb 17, 2011

NCJ 236223

John Laub
Director, National Institute of Justice

This report was prepared for the National Institute of Justice, U.S. Department of Justice, by the Office of Law Enforcement Standards of the National Institute of Standards and Technology under Interagency Agreement 2003–IJ–R–029.

The National Institute of Justice is a component of the Office of Justice Programs, which also includes the Bureau of Justice Assistance, the Bureau of Justice Statistics, the Office of Juvenile Justice and Delinquency Prevention, and the Office for Victims of Crime.

July 2011

Test Results for Digital Data Acquisition Tool:
Tableau TD1 Forensic Duplicator; Firmware Version 2.34 Feb 17, 2011

**National Institute of
Standards and Technology**
U.S. Department of Commerce

Contents

Introduction

The Computer Forensics Tool Testing (CFTT) program is a joint project of the National Institute of Justice (NIJ), the Department of Homeland Security (DHS), and the National Institute of Standards and Technology's Law Enforcement Standards Office and Information Technology Laboratory. CFTT is supported by other organizations, including the Federal Bureau of Investigation, the U.S. Department of Defense Cyber Crime Center, the U.S. Internal Revenue Service Criminal Investigation Division Electronic Crimes Program, and the U.S. Department of Homeland Security's Bureau of Immigration and Customs Enforcement, U.S. Customs and Border Protection and U.S. Secret Service. The objective of the CFTT program is to provide measurable assurance to practitioners, researchers and other applicable users that the tools used in computer forensics investigations provide accurate results. Accomplishing this requires the development of specifications and test methods for computer forensics tools and subsequent testing of specific tools against those specifications.

Test results provide the information necessary for developers to improve tools, users to make informed choices, and the legal community and others to understand the tools' capabilities. The CFTT approach to testing computer forensic tools is based on well-recognized methodologies for conformance and quality testing. The specifications and test methods are posted on the CFTT Web site (http://www.cftt.nist.gov/) for review and comment by the computer forensics community.

This document reports the results from testing the Tableau TD1 Forensic Duplicator, firmware version 2.34 Feb 17, 2011, against the *Digital Data Acquisition Tool Assertions and Test Plan Version 1.0*, available at the CFTT Web site (http://www.cftt.nist.gov/DA-ATP-pc-01.pdf).

Test results from other tools and the CFTT tool methodology can be found on NIJ's CFTT Web page, http://www.nij.gov/nij/topics/forensics/evidence/digital/standards/cftt.htm.

How to Read This Report

This report is divided into five sections. The first section is a summary of the results from the test runs and is sufficient for most readers to assess the suitability of the tool for the intended use. The remaining sections of the report describe how the tests were conducted, discuss any anomalies that were encountered and provide documentation of test case run details that support the report summary. Section 2 gives justification for the selection of test cases from the set of possible cases defined in the test plan for Digital Data Acquisition tools. The test cases are selected, in general, based on features offered by the tool. Section 3 describes in more depth any anomalies summarized in the first section. Section 4 lists hardware and software used to run the test cases with links to additional information about the items used. Section 5 contains a description of each test case run that lists all test assertions used in the test case, the expected result and the actual result. Please refer to the vendor's owner manual for guidance on using the tool.

Test Results for Digital Data Acquisition Tool

Tool Tested: TD1 Forensic Duplicator

Firmware Version: 2.34 Feb 17, 2011

Supplier: Guidance Software, Inc.

Address: W223 N608 Saratoga Drive
                    Waukesha, WI 53186

Tel: (262) 522-7890
Fax: (262) 522-7899

Email: support@tableau.com
WWW: http://www.tableau.com

1. Results Summary

The tool acquired source drives completely and accurately with the exception of the following: one case where a source drive containing faulty sectors was imaged, and two cases where source drives containing hidden sectors were imaged. In addition, there were two cases where the tool generated bogus alert messages in place of alerting the user to the presence of hidden sectors on the source drive.

The following behaviors were observed:
- When the tool was executed using the *fast* error recovery mode and faulty sectors were encountered, some readable sectors near the faulty sectors were replaced by zeros in the created clone (test case DA-09-FAST). This is the intended tool behavior as specified by the tool vendor.
- In two cases, DA-08-ATA28 (drive containing an HPA) and DA-08-DCO-ALT (drive containing a DCO), in place of alerting the user of hidden sectors on the source drive, the tool issued bogus alerts stating that the "Source disk may be blank." In case DA-08-ATA28, the tool removed the HPA from the source and all sectors were acquired. In case DA-08-DCO-ALT, the tool did not remove the DCO from the source and hidden sectors were not acquired.
- The tool does not automatically remove DCOs from source drives but is designed to alert the user when a DCO exists. A user may cancel the duplication process and manually remove the DCO using the "Disk Utilities" *Remove DCO & HPA* menu option. In cases DA-08-DCO and DA-08-DCO-ALT, the *Remove DCO & HPA* option was not exercised and sectors hidden by a DCO were not acquired. In case DA-08-DCO-ALT-SATA, the *Remove DCO & HPA* option was exercised to remove the DCO and all sectors were successfully acquired.

2. Test Case Selection

Test cases used to test disk imaging tools are defined in *Digital Data Acquisition Tool Assertions and Test Plan Version 1.0*. To test a tool, test cases are selected from the *Test Plan* document based on the features offered by the tool. Not all test cases or test assertions are appropriate for all tools. There is a core set of base cases (DA-06 and DA-08) that are executed for every tool tested. Tool features guide the selection of additional test cases. If a given tool implements a given feature, then the test cases linked to that feature are run. Table 1 lists the features available in the TD1 Forensic Duplicator and the linked test cases selected for execution. Table 2 lists the features not available in the TD1 Forensic Duplicator and the test cases not executed.

Table 1 Selected Test Cases

Supported Optional Feature	Cases Selected for Execution
Create a clone during acquisition	01
Create a truncated clone from a physical device	04
Base cases	06 & 08
Read error during acquisition	09
Create an image file in more than one format	10
Destination device switching	13

Table 2 Omitted Test Cases

Unsupported Optional Feature	Cases Omitted (Not Executed)
Create an unaligned clone from a digital source	02
Create cylinder aligned clones	03, 15, 21 & 23
Device I/O error generator available	05, 11 & 18
Create an image of a partition	07
Insufficient space for image file	12
Create a clone from an image file	14 & 17
Create a clone from a subset of an image file	16
Fill excess sectors on a clone acquisition	19
Fill excess sectors on a clone device	20, 21, 22 & 23
Detect a corrupted (or changed) image file	24 & 25
Convert an image file from one format to another	26

Some test cases have variant forms to accommodate parameters within test assertions. These variations cover the acquisition interface to the source drive and the way that sectors are hidden on a drive. Additional parameters that were varied between test cases were interface to target device, use of the *verify hash* setting, error recovery mode, and chunk (image file) size.

The following source access interfaces were tested: ATA28, ATA48, SATA28, SATA48 and ESATA. These are noted as variations on test cases DA-01, DA-06 and DA-08.

For test case DA-09, the TD1 Forensic Duplicator offers two error recovery modes for treating faulty sectors encountered on source media:

- *fast* – may skip some good sectors.
- *complete* – reads all readable sectors.

3. Results by Test Assertion

A test assertion is a verifiable statement about a single condition after an action is performed by the tool under test. A test case usually checks a group of assertions after the action of a single execution of the tool under test. Test assertions are defined and linked to test cases in *Digital Data Acquisition Tool Assertions and Test Plan Version 1.0*. Table 3 summarizes the test results for all the test cases by assertion. The column labeled **Assertions Tested** gives the text of each assertion. The column labeled **Tests** gives the number of test cases that use the given assertion. The column labeled **Anomaly** gives the section number in this report where any observed anomalies are discussed.

Table 3. Assertions Tested

Assertions Tested	Tests	Anomaly
AM-01 The tool uses access interface SRC-AI to access the digital source.	20	
AM-02 The tool acquires digital source DS.	20	
AM-03 The tool executes in execution environment XE.	20	
AM-04 If clone creation is specified, the tool creates a clone of the digital source.	6	
AM-05 If image file creation is specified, the tool creates an image file on file system type FS.	14	
AM-06 All visible sectors are acquired from the digital source.	20	3.1
AM-07 All hidden sectors are acquired from the digital source.	5	3.2
AM-08 All sectors acquired from the digital source are acquired accurately.	20	
AM-09 If unresolved errors occur while reading from the selected digital source, the tool notifies the user of the error type and location within the digital source.	2	
AM-10 If unresolved errors occur while reading from the selected digital source, the tool uses a benign fill in the destination object in place of the inaccessible data.	2	
AO-01 If the tool creates an image file, the data represented by the image file is the same as the data acquired by the tool.	14	
AO-02 If an image file format is specified, the tool creates an image file in the specified format.	1	
AO-04 If the tool is creating an image file and there is insufficient space on the image destination device to contain the image file, the tool shall notify the user.	1	
AO-05 If the tool creates a multi-file image of a requested size, then all the individual files shall be no larger than the requested size.	14	

Assertions Tested	Tests	Anomaly
AO-10 If there is insufficient space to contain all files of a multi-file image, and if destination device switching is supported, the image is continued on another device.	1	
AO-11 If requested, a clone is created during an acquisition of a digital source.	6	
AO-13 A clone is created using access interface DST-AI to write to the clone device.	6	
AO-14 If an unaligned clone is created, each sector written to the clone is accurately written to the same disk address on the clone that the sector occupied on the digital source.	6	
AO-17 If requested, any excess sectors on a clone destination device are not modified.	4	
AO-19 If there is insufficient space to create a complete clone, a truncated clone is created using all available sectors of the clone device.	1	
AO-20 If a truncated clone is created, the tool notifies the user.	1	
AO-23 If the tool logs any log significant information, the information is accurately recorded in the log file.	20	3.3
AO-24 If the tool executes in a forensically safe execution environment, the digital source is unchanged by the acquisition process.	20	

Two test assertions only apply in special circumstances. The assertion AO-22 is checked only for tools that create block hashes. The assertion AO-24 is only checked if the tool is executed in a run time environment that does not modify attached storage devices, such as MS DOS. In normal operation, an imaging tool is used in conjunction with a write block device to protect the source drive; however, a blocker was not used during the tests so that assertion AO-24 could be checked. Table 4 lists the assertions that were not tested, usually due to the tool not supporting some optional feature, e.g., creation of cylinder aligned clones.

Table 4 Assertions Not Tested

Assertions Not Tested
AO-03 If there is an error while writing the image file, the tool notifies the user.
AO-06 If the tool performs an image file integrity check on an image file that has not been changed since the file was created, the tool shall notify the user that the image file has not been changed.
AO-07 If the tool performs an image file integrity check on an image file that has been changed since the file was created, the tool shall notify the user that the image file has been changed.
AO-08 If the tool performs an image file integrity check on an image file that has been changed since the file was created, the tool shall notify the user of the affected locations.
AO-09 If the tool converts a source image file from one format to a target image file in another format, the acquired data represented in the target image file is the same as the

Assertions Not Tested
acquired data in the source image file.
AO-12 If requested, a clone is created from an image file.
AO-15 If an aligned clone is created, each sector within a contiguous span of sectors from the source is accurately written to the same disk address on the clone device relative to the start of the span as the sector occupied on the original digital source. A span of sectors is defined to be either a mountable partition or a contiguous sequence of sectors not part of a mountable partition. Extended partitions, which may contain both mountable partitions and unallocated sectors, are not mountable partitions.
AO-16 If a subset of an image or acquisition is specified, all the subset is cloned.
AO-18 If requested, a benign fill is written to excess sectors of a clone.
AO-21 If there is a write error during clone creation, the tool notifies the user.
AO-22 If requested, the tool calculates block hashes for a specified block size during an acquisition for each block acquired from the digital source.

3.1 Acquisition of Faulty Sectors

The Tableau TD1 Forensic Duplicator (firmware version 2.34 Feb 17, 2011) offers two error recovery modes for treating faulty sectors encountered on source media:

- *fast* – may skip some readable sectors near faulty sectors.
- *complete* – reads all readable sectors.

For test case DA-09-FAST, the *fast* error recovery mode was specified and readable sectors in the same 128-sector imaging block as faulty sectors were skipped and replaced by zeros in the created clone. For test case DA-09-COMPLETE, the *complete* error recovery mode was specified and all readable sectors were acquired. This is the behavior intended for the tool by the tool vendor.

3.2 DCO Hidden Sector Tests

The tool does not automatically remove DCOs from source drives but is designed to alert the user when a DCO exists. A user may cancel the duplication process and manually remove the DCO using a Disk Utilities option. In cases DA-08-DCO and DA-08-DCO-ALT, the Disk Utilities option was not exercised and sectors hidden by a DCO were not acquired; in case DA-08-DCO-ALT-SATA, the Disk Utilities option was exercised to remove the DCO and all sectors were successfully acquired.

3.3 Bogus Error Messages

The tool is designed to warn the user prior to the start of an acquisition when a source drive contains hidden sectors (i.e., an HPA or DCO). In two cases, DA-08-ATA28 and DA-08-DCO-ALT, in place of alerting the user of hidden sectors on the source drive the tool issued bogus alerts stating that the "Source disk may be blank." In case DA-08-ATA28, a source drive containing an HPA was imaged. The tool automatically removed the HPA and acquired all visible and hidden sectors. In case DA-08-DCO-ALT, a source drive containing a DCO was imaged. In this case, visible sectors were acquired but sectors hidden by a DCO were not.

4. Testing Environment

The tests were run in the NIST CFTT lab. This section describes using the support software and notes on test hardware.

4.1 Support Software

A package of programs to support test analysis, FS-TST Release 2.0, was used. The software can be obtained from http://www.cftt.nist.gov/diskimaging/fs-tst20.zip.

4.2 Test Drive Creation

There are three ways that a hard drive may be used in a tool test case: as a source drive that is imaged by the tool, as a media drive that contains image files created by the tool under test, or as a destination drive on which the tool under test creates a clone of the source drive. In addition to the operating system drive formatting tools, some tools (**diskwipe** and **diskhash**) from the FS-TST package are used to set up test drives.

To set up a media drive, the drive is formatted with one of the supported file systems. A media drive may be used in several test cases.

The setup of most source drives follows the same general procedure, but there are several steps that may be varied depending on the needs of the test case.
1. The drive is filled with known data by the **diskwipe** program from FS-TST. The **diskwipe** program writes the sector address to each sector in both C/H/S and LBA format. The remainder of the sector bytes is set to a constant fill value unique for each drive. The fill value is noted in the **diskwipe** tool log file.
2. The drive may be formatted with partitions as required for the test case.
3. An operating system may optionally be installed.
4. A set of reference hashes is created by the FS-TST **diskhash** tool. These include both SHA1 and MD5 hashes. In addition to full drive hashes, hashes of each partition may also be computed.
5. If the drive is intended for hidden area tests (DA-08), an HPA, a DCO or both may be created. The **diskhash** tool is then used to calculate reference hashes of just the visible sectors of the drive.

The source drives for DA-09 are created such that there is a consistent set of faulty sectors on the drive. Each of these source drives is initialized with **diskwipe** and then their faulty sectors are activated. For each of these source drives, a second drive of the same size with the same content as the faulty sector drive but with no faulty sectors serves as a reference drive for images made from the faulty drive.

To set up a destination drive, the drive is filled with known data by the **diskwipe** program from FS-TST. Partitions may be created if the test case involves restoring from the image of a logical acquire.

4.3 Test Drive Analysis

For test cases that create a clone of a physical device (e.g., DA-01, DA-04), the destination drive is compared to the source drive with the **diskcmp** program from the FS-TST package. For test cases that create a clone of a logical device (i.e., a partition, e.g., DA-02, DA-20), the destination partition is compared to the source partition with the **partcmp** program. For a destination created from an image file (e.g., DA-14), the destination is compared using either **diskcmp** (for physical device clones) or **partcmp** (for partition clones) to the source that was acquired to create the image file. Both **diskcmp** and **partcmp** note differences between the source and destination. If the destination is larger than the source, it is scanned and the excess destination sectors are categorized as either undisturbed (still containing the fill pattern written by **diskwipe**), zero filled or changed to something else.

For test case DA-09, imaging a drive with known faulty sectors, the program **anabad** is used to compare the faulty sector reference drive to a cloned version of the faulty sector drive.

For test cases such as DA-06 and DA-07, any acquisition hash computed by the tool under test is compared to the reference hash of the source to check that the source is completely and accurately acquired.

4.4 Note on Test Drives

The testing uses several test drives from a variety of vendors. The drives are identified by an external label that consists of a 2-digit hexadecimal value and an optional tag (e.g., 25-SATA). The combination of hex value and tag serves as a unique identifier for each drive. The 2-digit hex value is used by the FS-TST **diskwipe** program as a sector fill value. The FS-TST compare tools, **diskcmp** and **partcmp**, count sectors that are filled with the source and destination fill values on a destination that is larger than the original source.

5. Test Results

The main item of interest for interpreting the test results is determining the conformance of the device with the test assertions. Conformance with each assertion tested by a given test case is evaluated by examining the **Log Highlights** box of the test case details.

5.1 Test Results Report Key

A summary of the actual test results is presented in this report. The following table presents a description of each section of the test report summary. The Tester Name, Test Host, Test Date, Drives, Source Setup and Log Highlights sections for each test case are populated by excerpts taken from the log files produced by the tool under test and the FS-TST tools that were executed in support of test case setup and analysis.

Heading	Description
First Line:	Test case ID, name and version of tool tested.
Case Summary:	Test case summary from *Digital Data Acquisition Tool Assertions and Test Plan Version 1.0.*

Heading	Description
Assertions:	The test assertions applicable to the test case, selected from *Digital Data Acquisition Tool Assertions and Test Plan Version 1.0.*
Tester Name:	Name or initials of person executing test procedure.
Test Host:	Host computer executing the test.
Test Date:	Time and date that test was started.
Drives:	Source drive (the drive acquired), destination drive (if a clone is created) and media drive (to contain a created image).
Source Setup:	Layout of partitions on the source drive and the expected hash of the drive.
Log Highlights:	Information extracted from various log files to illustrate conformance or nonconformance to the test assertions.
Results:	Expected and actual results for each assertion tested.
Analysis:	Whether or not the expected results were achieved.

5.2 Test Details

5.2.1 DA-01-ATA28

Test Case DA-01-ATA28 Tableau TD1 Version 2.34	
Case Summary:	DA-01 Acquire a physical device using access interface AI to an unaligned clone.
Assertions:	AM-01 The tool uses access interface SRC-AI to access the digital source. AM-02 The tool acquires digital source DS. AM-03 The tool executes in execution environment XE. AM-04 If clone creation is specified, the tool creates a clone of the digital source. AM-06 All visible sectors are acquired from the digital source. AM-08 All sectors acquired from the digital source are acquired accurately. AO-11 If requested, a clone is created during an acquisition of a digital source. AO-13 A clone is created using access interface DST-AI to write to the clone device. AO-14 If an unaligned clone is created, each sector written to the clone is accurately written to the same disk address on the clone that the sector occupied on the digital source. AO-17 If requested, any excess sectors on a clone destination device are not modified. AO-22 If requested, the tool calculates block hashes for a specified block size during an acquisition for each block acquired from the digital source. AO-23 If the tool logs any log significant information, the information is accurately recorded in the log file. AO-24 If the tool executes in a forensically safe execution environment, the digital source is unchanged by the acquisition process.
Tester Name:	brl
Test Host:	TD1
Test Date:	Mon Mar 21 10:48:49 2011
Drives:	src(01-IDE) dst (58-IDE) other (none)

Source Setup:	src hash (SHA1): < A48BB5665D6DC57C22DB68E2F723DA9AA8DF82B9 >
	 src hash (MD5): < F458F673894753FA6A0EC8B8EC63848E >
	 78165360 total sectors (40020664320 bytes)
	 Model (0BB-00JHC0) serial # (WD-WMAMC74171)
	   N Start LBA Length Start C/H/S End C/H/S boot Partition type
	   1 P 000000063 020980827 0000/001/01 1023/254/63 0C Fat32X
	   2 X 020980890 057175335 1023/000/01 1023/254/63 0F extended
	   3 S 000000063 000032067 1023/001/01 1023/254/63 01 Fat12

```
 4 x 000032130 002104515 1023/000/01 1023/254/63        05 extended
 5 S 000000063 002104452 1023/001/01 1023/254/63        06 Fat16
 6 x 002136645 004192965 1023/000/01 1023/254/63        05 extended
 7 S 000000063 004192902 1023/001/01 1023/254/63        16 other
 8 x 006329610 008401995 1023/000/01 1023/254/63        05 extended
 9 S 000000063 008401932 1023/001/01 1023/254/63        0B Fat32
10 x 014731605 010490445 1023/000/01 1023/254/63        05 extended
11 S 000000063 010490382 1023/001/01 1023/254/63        83 Linux
12 x 025222050 004209030 1023/000/01 1023/254/63        05 extended
13 S 000000063 004208967 1023/001/01 1023/254/63        82 Linux swap
14 x 029431080 027744255 1023/000/01 1023/254/63        05 extended
15 S 000000063 027744192 1023/001/01 1023/254/63        07 NTFS
16 S 000000000 000000000 0000/000/00 0000/000/00        00 empty entry
17 P 000000000 000000000 0000/000/00 0000/000/00        00 empty entry
18 P 000000000 000000000 0000/000/00 0000/000/00        00 empty entry
```

Log Highlights:	
	====== Destination drive setup ====== 117231408 sectors wiped with 58 ====== Comparison of original to clone drive ====== Sectors compared: 78165360 Sectors match: 78165360 Sectors differ: 0 Bytes differ: 0 Diffs range Source (78165360) has 39066048 fewer sectors than destination (117231408) Zero fill: 0 Src Byte fill (01): 0 Dst Byte fill (58): 39066048 Other fill: 0 Other no fill: 0 Zero fill range: Src fill range: Dst fill range: 78165360-117231407 Other fill range: Other not filled range: 0 source read errors, 0 destination read errors ====== Tool Settings ====== dst-interface ATA28 verify-hash on ======== Excerpt from Log file ======== Task: Disk to Disk Case: DA-01-ATA28 # of sectors acquired: 78,165,360 (40.0 GB) Source hash: SHA1: a48bb5665d6dc57c22db68e2f723da9aa8df82b9 MD5 : f458f673894753fa6a0ec8b8ec63848e Verification hash: SHA1: a48bb5665d6dc57c22db68e2f723da9aa8df82b9 MD5 : f458f673894753fa6a0ec8b8ec63848e ======== End of Excerpt from Log file ======== ====== Source drive rehash ====== Rehash (SHA1) of source: A48BB5665D6DC57C22DB68E2F723DA9AA8DF82B9

Results:		
	Assertion & Expected Result	**Actual Result**
	AM-01 Source acquired using interface AI.	as expected
	AM-02 Source is type DS.	as expected
	AM-03 Execution environment is XE.	as expected
	AM-04 A clone is created.	as expected
	AM-06 All visible sectors acquired.	as expected
	AM-08 All sectors accurately acquired.	as expected
	AO-11 A clone is created during acquisition.	as expected

Test Case DA-01-ATA28 Tableau TD1 Version 2.34		
	AO-13 Clone created using interface AI.	as expected
	AO-14 An unaligned clone is created.	as expected
	AO-17 Excess sectors are unchanged.	as expected
	AO-22 Tool calculates hashes by block.	option not available
	AO-23 Logged information is correct.	as expected
	AO-24 Source is unchanged by acquisition.	as expected
Analysis:	Expected results achieved	

5.2.2 DA-01-ATA48

Test Case DA-01-ATA48 Tableau TD1 Version 2.34	
Case Summary:	DA-01 Acquire a physical device using access interface AI to an unaligned clone.
Assertions:	AM-01 The tool uses access interface SRC-AI to access the digital source. AM-02 The tool acquires digital source DS. AM-03 The tool executes in execution environment XE. AM-04 If clone creation is specified, the tool creates a clone of the digital source. AM-06 All visible sectors are acquired from the digital source. AM-08 All sectors acquired from the digital source are acquired accurately. AO-11 If requested, a clone is created during an acquisition of a digital source. AO-13 A clone is created using access interface DST-AI to write to the clone device. AO-14 If an unaligned clone is created, each sector written to the clone is accurately written to the same disk address on the clone that the sector occupied on the digital source. AO-17 If requested, any excess sectors on a clone destination device are not modified. AO-22 If requested, the tool calculates block hashes for a specified block size during an acquisition for each block acquired from the digital source. AO-23 If the tool logs any log significant information, the information is accurately recorded in the log file. AO-24 If the tool executes in a forensically safe execution environment, the digital source is unchanged by the acquisition process.
Tester Name:	brl
Test Host:	TD1
Test Date:	Mon Mar 21 11:51:23 2011
Drives:	src(4C) dst (46-SATA) other (none)
Source Setup:	src hash (SHA1): < 8FF620D2BEDCCAFE8412EDAAD56C8554F872EFBF > src hash (MD5): < D10F763B56D4CEBA2D1311C61F9FB382 > 390721968 total sectors (200049647616 bytes) 24320/254/63 (max cyl/hd values) 24321/255/63 (number of cyl/hd) IDE disk: Model (WDC WD2000JB-00KFA0) serial # (WD-WMAMR1031111) N Start LBA Length Start C/H/S End C/H/S boot Partition type 1 P 000000063 390700737 0000/001/01 1023/254/63 Boot 07 NTFS 2 P 000000000 000000000 0000/000/00 0000/000/00 00 empty entry 3 P 000000000 000000000 0000/000/00 0000/000/00 00 empty entry 4 P 000000000 000000000 0000/000/00 0000/000/00 00 empty entry 1 390700737 sectors 200038777344 bytes
Log Highlights:	====== Destination drive setup ====== 488397168 sectors wiped with 46 ====== Comparison of original to clone drive ====== Sectors compared: 390721968 Sectors match: 390721968 Sectors differ: 0 Bytes differ: 0 Diffs range Source (390721968) has 97675200 fewer sectors than destination (488397168) Zero fill: 0 Src Byte fill (4C): 0 Dst Byte fill (46): 97675200 Other fill: 0 Other no fill: 0 Zero fill range: Src fill range: Dst fill range: 390721968-488397167 Other fill range: Other not filled range: 0 source read errors, 0 destination read errors ====== Tool Settings ======

```
dst-interface SATA48
verify-hash off


======== Excerpt from Log file ========
Task: Disk to Disk
Case:  DA-01-ATA48
# of sectors acquired: 390,721,968 (200.0 GB)
Source hash:
 SHA1: 8ff620d2bedccafe8412edaad56c8554f872efbf
 MD5 : d10f763b56d4ceba2d1311c61f9fb382

======== End of Excerpt from Log file ========

====== Source drive rehash ======
Rehash (SHA1) of source: 8FF620D2BEDCCAFE8412EDAAD56C8554F872EFBF
```

Results:

Assertion & Expected Result	Actual Result
AM-01 Source acquired using interface AI.	as expected
AM-02 Source is type DS.	as expected
AM-03 Execution environment is XE.	as expected
AM-04 A clone is created.	as expected
AM-06 All visible sectors acquired.	as expected
AM-08 All sectors accurately acquired.	as expected
AO-11 A clone is created during acquisition.	as expected
AO-13 Clone created using interface AI.	as expected
AO-14 An unaligned clone is created.	as expected
AO-17 Excess sectors are unchanged.	as expected
AO-22 Tool calculates hashes by block.	option not available
AO-23 Logged information is correct.	as expected
AO-24 Source is unchanged by acquisition.	as expected

Analysis: Expected results achieved

5.2.3 DA-01-ESATA

Test Case DA-01-ESATA Tableau TD1 Version 2.34	
Case Summary:	DA-01 Acquire a physical device using access interface AI to an unaligned clone.
Assertions:	AM-01 The tool uses access interface SRC-AI to access the digital source.
	AM-02 The tool acquires digital source DS.
	AM-03 The tool executes in execution environment XE.
	AM-04 If clone creation is specified, the tool creates a clone of the digital source.
	AM-06 All visible sectors are acquired from the digital source.
	AM-08 All sectors acquired from the digital source are acquired accurately.
	AO-11 If requested, a clone is created during an acquisition of a digital source.
	AO-13 A clone is created using access interface DST-AI to write to the clone device.
	AO-14 If an unaligned clone is created, each sector written to the clone is accurately written to the same disk address on the clone that the sector occupied on the digital source.
	AO-17 If requested, any excess sectors on a clone destination device are not modified.
	AO-22 If requested, the tool calculates block hashes for a specified block size during an acquisition for each block acquired from the digital source.
	AO-23 If the tool logs any log significant information, the information is accurately recorded in the log file.
	AO-24 If the tool executes in a forensically safe execution environment, the digital source is unchanged by the acquisition process.
Tester Name:	brl
Test Host:	TD1
Test Date:	Tue Mar 22 10:14:20 2011
Drives:	src(07-SATA) dst (26-IDE) other (none)
Source Setup:	src hash (SHA256): < CE65C4A3C3164D3EBAD58D33BB2415D29E260E1F88DC5A131B1C4C9C2945B8A9 > src hash (SHA1): < 655E9BDDB36A3F9C5C4CC8BF32B8C5B41AF9F52E > src hash (MD5): < 2EAF712DAD80F66E30DEA00365B4579B > 156301488 total sectors (80026361856 bytes) Model (WDC WD800JD-32HK) serial # (WD-WMAJ91510044) N Start LBA Length Start C/H/S End C/H/S boot Partition type 1 P 000000063 156280257 0000/001/01 1023/254/63 Boot 07 NTFS 2 P 000000000 000000000 0000/000/00 0000/000/00 00 empty entry 3 P 000000000 000000000 0000/000/00 0000/000/00 00 empty entry 4 P 000000000 000000000 0000/000/00 0000/000/00 00 empty entry 1 156280257 sectors 80015491584 bytes
Log Highlights:	====== Destination drive setup ====== 312581808 sectors wiped with 26 ====== Comparison of original to clone drive ====== Sectors compared: 156301488 Sectors match: 156301488 Sectors differ: 0 Bytes differ: 0 Diffs range Source (156301488) has 156280320 fewer sectors than destination (312581808) Zero fill: 0 Src Byte fill (07): 0 Dst Byte fill (26): 156280320 Other fill: 0 Other no fill: 0 Zero fill range: Src fill range: Dst fill range: 156301488-312581807 Other fill range: Other not filled range: 0 source read errors, 0 destination read errors

Test Case DA-01-ESATA Tableau TD1 Version 2.34

```
====== Tool Settings ======
dst-interface ATA48
verify-hash off


======== Excerpt from Log file ========
Task: Disk to Disk
Case:  DA-01-ESATA
# of sectors acquired: 156,301,488 (80.0 GB)
Source hash:
 SHA1: 655e9bddb36a3f9c5c4cc8bf32b8c5b41af9f52e
 MD5 : 2eaf712dad80f66e30dea00365b4579b

======== End of Excerpt from Log file ========

====== Source drive rehash ======
Rehash (SHA1) of source: 655E9BDDB36A3F9C5C4CC8BF32B8C5B41AF9F52E
```

Results:

Assertion & Expected Result	Actual Result
AM-01 Source acquired using interface AI.	as expected
AM-02 Source is type DS.	as expected
AM-03 Execution environment is XE.	as expected
AM-04 A clone is created.	as expected
AM-06 All visible sectors acquired.	as expected
AM-08 All sectors accurately acquired.	as expected
AO-11 A clone is created during acquisition.	as expected
AO-13 Clone created using interface AI.	as expected
AO-14 An unaligned clone is created.	as expected
AO-17 Excess sectors are unchanged.	as expected
AO-22 Tool calculates hashes by block.	option not available
AO-23 Logged information is correct.	as expected
AO-24 Source is unchanged by acquisition.	as expected

Analysis: Expected results achieved

5.2.4 DA-01-SATA28

Test Case DA-01-SATA28 Tableau TD1 Version 2.34	
Case Summary:	DA-01 Acquire a physical device using access interface AI to an unaligned clone.
Assertions:	AM-01 The tool uses access interface SRC-AI to access the digital source. AM-02 The tool acquires digital source DS. AM-03 The tool executes in execution environment XE. AM-04 If clone creation is specified, the tool creates a clone of the digital source. AM-06 All visible sectors are acquired from the digital source. AM-08 All sectors acquired from the digital source are acquired accurately. AO-11 If requested, a clone is created during an acquisition of a digital source. AO-13 A clone is created using access interface DST-AI to write to the clone device. AO-14 If an unaligned clone is created, each sector written to the clone is accurately written to the same disk address on the clone that the sector occupied on the digital source. AO-17 If requested, any excess sectors on a clone destination device are not modified. AO-22 If requested, the tool calculates block hashes for a specified block size during an acquisition for each block acquired from the digital source. AO-23 If the tool logs any log significant information, the information is accurately recorded in the log file. AO-24 If the tool executes in a forensically safe execution environment, the digital source is unchanged by the acquisition process.
Tester Name:	brl
Test Host:	TD1
Test Date:	Mon Mar 21 13:52:27 2011
Drives:	src(07-SATA) dst (22-IDE) other (none)

Source Setup:	src hash (SHA256): <
	CE65C4A3C3164D3EBAD58D33BB2415D29E260E1F88DC5A131B1C4C9C2945B8A9 >
	src hash (SHA1): < 655E9BDDB36A3F9C5C4CC8BF32B8C5B41AF9F52E >
	src hash (MD5): < 2EAF712DAD80F66E30DEA00365B4579B >
	156301488 total sectors (80026361856 bytes)
	Model (WDC WD800JD-32HK) serial # (WD-WMAJ91510044)
	  N Start LBA Length Start C/H/S End C/H/S boot Partition type
	  1 P 000000063 156280257 0000/001/01 1023/254/63 Boot 07 NTFS
	  2 P 000000000 000000000 0000/000/00 0000/000/00 00 empty entry
	  3 P 000000000 000000000 0000/000/00 0000/000/00 00 empty entry
	  4 P 000000000 000000000 0000/000/00 0000/000/00 00 empty entry
	1 156280257 sectors 80015491584 bytes

Log Highlights:	====== Destination drive setup ====== 195813072 sectors wiped with 22 ====== Comparison of original to clone drive ====== Sectors compared: 156301488 Sectors match: 156301488 Sectors differ: 0 Bytes differ: 0 Diffs range Source (156301488) has 39511584 fewer sectors than destination (195813072) Zero fill: 0 Src Byte fill (07): 0 Dst Byte fill (22): 39511584 Other fill: 0 Other no fill: 0 Zero fill range: Src fill range: Dst fill range: 156301488-195813071 Other fill range: Other not filled range: 0 source read errors, 0 destination read errors

```
Test Case DA-01-SATA28 Tableau TD1 Version 2.34
```

| | ====== Tool Settings ======
dst-interface ATA28
verify-hash on

======== Excerpt from Log file ========
Task: Disk to Disk
Case: DA-01-SATA28
# of sectors acquired: 156,301,488 (80.0 GB)
Source hash:
 SHA1: 655e9bddb36a3f9c5c4cc8bf32b8c5b41af9f52e
 MD5 : 2eaf712dad80f66e30dea00365b4579b
Verification hash:
 SHA1: 655e9bddb36a3f9c5c4cc8bf32b8c5b41af9f52e
 MD5 : 2eaf712dad80f66e30dea00365b4579b

======== End of Excerpt from Log file ========

====== Source drive rehash ======
Rehash (SHA1) of source: 655E9BDDB36A3F9C5C4CC8BF32B8C5B41AF9F52E |
| Results: | |

Assertion & Expected Result	Actual Result
AM-01 Source acquired using interface AI.	as expected
AM-02 Source is type DS.	as expected
AM-03 Execution environment is XE.	as expected
AM-04 A clone is created.	as expected
AM-06 All visible sectors acquired.	as expected
AM-08 All sectors accurately acquired.	as expected
AO-11 A clone is created during acquisition.	as expected
AO-13 Clone created using interface AI.	as expected
AO-14 An unaligned clone is created.	as expected
AO-17 Excess sectors are unchanged.	as expected
AO-22 Tool calculates hashes by block.	option not available
AO-23 Logged information is correct.	as expected
AO-24 Source is unchanged by acquisition.	as expected

Analysis:	Expected results achieved

5.2.5 DA-01-SATA48

Test Case DA-01-SATA48 Tableau TD1 Version 2.34	
Case Summary:	DA-01 Acquire a physical device using access interface AI to an unaligned clone.
Assertions:	AM-01 The tool uses access interface SRC-AI to access the digital source. AM-02 The tool acquires digital source DS. AM-03 The tool executes in execution environment XE. AM-04 If clone creation is specified, the tool creates a clone of the digital source. AM-06 All visible sectors are acquired from the digital source. AM-08 All sectors acquired from the digital source are acquired accurately. AO-11 If requested, a clone is created during an acquisition of a digital source. AO-13 A clone is created using access interface DST-AI to write to the clone device. AO-14 If an unaligned clone is created, each sector written to the clone is accurately written to the same disk address on the clone that the sector occupied on the digital source. AO-17 If requested, any excess sectors on a clone destination device are not modified. AO-22 If requested, the tool calculates block hashes for a specified block size during an acquisition for each block acquired from the digital source. AO-23 If the tool logs any log significant information, the information is accurately recorded in the log file. AO-24 If the tool executes in a forensically safe execution environment, the digital source is unchanged by the acquisition process.
Tester Name:	brl
Test Host:	TD1
Test Date:	Mon Mar 21 13:22:33 2011
Drives:	src(0D-SATA) dst (44-SATA) other (none)
Source Setup:	src hash (SHA1): < BAAD80E8781E55F2E3EF528CA73BD41D228C1377 > src hash (MD5): < 1FA7C3CBE60EB9E89863DED2411E40C9 > 488397168 total sectors (250059350016 bytes) 30400/254/63 (max cyl/hd values) 30401/255/63 (number of cyl/hd) Model (WDC WD2500JD-22F) serial # (WD-WMAEH2678216) N Start LBA Length Start C/H/S End C/H/S boot Partition type 1 P 000000063 488375937 0000/001/01 1023/254/63 Boot 07 NTFS 2 P 000000000 000000000 0000/000/00 0000/000/00 00 empty entry 3 P 000000000 000000000 0000/000/00 0000/000/00 00 empty entry 4 P 000000000 000000000 0000/000/00 0000/000/00 00 empty entry 1 488375937 sectors 250048479744 bytes
Log Highlights:	====== Destination drive setup ====== 488397168 sectors wiped with 44 ====== Comparison of original to clone drive ====== Sectors compared: 488397168 Sectors match: 488397168 Sectors differ: 0 Bytes differ: 0 Diffs range 0 source read errors, 0 destination read errors ====== Tool Settings ====== dst-interface SATA48 verify-hash off ======== Excerpt from Log file ======== Task: Disk to Disk Case: DA-01-SATA48 # of sectors acquired: 488,397,168 (250.0 GB) Source hash: SHA1: baad80e8781e55f2e3ef528ca73bd41d228c1377 MD5 : 1fa7c3cbe60eb9e89863ded2411e40c9

Test Case DA-01-SATA48 Tableau TD1 Version 2.34	
	======== End of Excerpt from Log file ======== ====== Source drive rehash ====== Rehash (SHA1) of source: BAAD80E8781E55F2E3EF528CA73BD41D228C1377
Results:	

Assertion & Expected Result	Actual Result
AM-01 Source acquired using interface AI.	as expected
AM-02 Source is type DS.	as expected
AM-03 Execution environment is XE.	as expected
AM-04 A clone is created.	as expected
AM-06 All visible sectors acquired.	as expected
AM-08 All sectors accurately acquired.	as expected
AO-11 A clone is created during acquisition.	as expected
AO-13 Clone created using interface AI.	as expected
AO-14 An unaligned clone is created.	as expected
AO-17 Excess sectors are unchanged.	as expected
AO-22 Tool calculates hashes by block.	option not available
AO-23 Logged information is correct.	as expected
AO-24 Source is unchanged by acquisition.	as expected

Analysis:	Expected results achieved

5.2.6 DA-04

Test Case DA-04 Tableau TD1 Version 2.34	
Case Summary:	DA-04 Acquire a physical device to a truncated clone.
Assertions:	AM-01 The tool uses access interface SRC-AI to access the digital source. AM-02 The tool acquires digital source DS. AM-03 The tool executes in execution environment XE. AM-04 If clone creation is specified, the tool creates a clone of the digital source. AM-06 All visible sectors are acquired from the digital source. AM-08 All sectors acquired from the digital source are acquired accurately. AO-11 If requested, a clone is created during an acquisition of a digital source. AO-13 A clone is created using access interface DST-AI to write to the clone device. AO-14 If an unaligned clone is created, each sector written to the clone is accurately written to the same disk address on the clone that the sector occupied on the digital source. AO-19 If there is insufficient space to create a complete clone, a truncated clone is created using all available sectors of the clone device. AO-20 If a truncated clone is created, the tool notifies the user. AO-22 If requested, the tool calculates block hashes for a specified block size during an acquisition for each block acquired from the digital source. AO-23 If the tool logs any log significant information, the information is accurately recorded in the log file. AO-24 If the tool executes in a forensically safe execution environment, the digital source is unchanged by the acquisition process.
Tester Name:	brl
Test Host:	TD1
Test Date:	Tue Mar 22 10:36:04 2011
Drives:	src(41) dst (90) other (none)
Source Setup:	src hash (SHA256): < FBF3AA21489653D880FFAE71449A9F7E8EE4F56A6C3BF58A3A3FFB13203F1B1D > src hash (SHA1): < 15CAA1A307271160D8372668BF8A03FC45A51CC9 > src hash (MD5): < 0A6A8EF78BDC14E2026710D8CCB5607C > 78125000 total sectors (40000000000 bytes) 65534/015/63 (max cyl/hd values) 65535/016/63 (number of cyl/hd) IDE disk: Model (WDC WD400BB-75JHC0) serial # (WD-WMAMC4658355) N Start LBA Length Start C/H/S End C/H/S boot Partition type 1 P 000000063 078107967 0000/001/01 1023/254/63 Boot 07 NTFS 2 P 000000000 000000000 0000/000/00 0000/000/00 00 empty entry 3 P 000000000 000000000 0000/000/00 0000/000/00 00 empty entry 4 P 000000000 000000000 0000/000/00 0000/000/00 00 empty entry 1 078107967 sectors 39991279104 bytes
Log Highlights:	====== Destination drive setup ====== 58633344 sectors wiped with 90 ====== Tool Message ====== **ALERT** Destination disk is too small. ====== Tool Settings ====== dst-interface ATA28 verify-hash off ======== Excerpt from Log file ======== No logfile created ======== End of Excerpt from Log file ======== ====== Source drive rehash ====== Rehash (SHA1) of source: 15CAA1A307271160D8372668BF8A03FC45A51CC9
Results:	

Test Case DA-04 Tableau TD1 Version 2.34		
	Assertion & Expected Result	**Actual Result**
	AM-01 Source acquired using interface AI.	as expected
	AM-02 Source is type DS.	as expected
	AM-03 Execution environment is XE.	as expected
	AM-04 A clone is created.	as expected
	AM-06 All visible sectors acquired.	as expected
	AM-08 All sectors accurately acquired.	as expected
	AO-11 A clone is created during acquisition.	as expected
	AO-13 Clone created using interface AI.	as expected
	AO-14 An unaligned clone is created.	as expected
	AO-19 Truncated clone is created.	as expected
	AO-20 User notified that clone is truncated.	as expected
	AO-22 Tool calculates hashes by block.	option not available
	AO-23 Logged information is correct.	as expected
	AO-24 Source is unchanged by acquisition.	as expected
Analysis:	Expected results achieved	

5.2.7 DA-06-ATA28

Test Case DA-06-ATA28 Tableau TD1 Version 2.34	
Case Summary:	DA-06 Acquire a physical device using access interface AI to an image file.
Assertions:	AM-01 The tool uses access interface SRC-AI to access the digital source. AM-02 The tool acquires digital source DS. AM-03 The tool executes in execution environment XE. AM-05 If image file creation is specified, the tool creates an image file on file system type FS. AM-06 All visible sectors are acquired from the digital source. AM-08 All sectors acquired from the digital source are acquired accurately. AO-01 If the tool creates an image file, the data represented by the image file is the same as the data acquired by the tool. AO-05 If the tool creates a multi-file image of a requested size then all the individual files shall be no larger than the requested size. AO-22 If requested, the tool calculates block hashes for a specified block size during an acquisition for each block acquired from the digital source. AO-23 If the tool logs any log significant information, the information is accurately recorded in the log file. AO-24 If the tool executes in a forensically safe execution environment, the digital source is unchanged by the acquisition process.
Tester Name:	brl
Test Host:	TD1
Test Date:	Tue Mar 22 10:54:13 2011
Drives:	src(43) dst (none) other (78-SATA-SSD)

Source Setup:	src hash (SHA256): <
	2658F47603DE6B1D883B64823E9733F578658D08D06A4BB8C053C4F57BDC615E >
	src hash (SHA1): < 888E2E7F7AD237DC7A732281DD93F325065E5871 >
	src hash (MD5): < BC39C3F7EE7A50E77B9BA1E65A5AEEF7 >
	78125000 total sectors (40000000000 bytes)
	Model (0BB-75JHC0) serial # (WD-WMAMC46588)<pre> N Start LBA Length Start C/H/S End C/H/S boot Partition type
	  1 P 000000063 020980827 0000/001/01 1023/254/63 0C Fat32X
	  2 X 020980890 057143205 1023/000/01 1023/254/63 0F extended
	  3 S 000000063 000032067 1023/001/01 1023/254/63 01 Fat12
	  4 x 000032130 002104515 1023/000/01 1023/254/63 05 extended
	  5 S 000000063 002104452 1023/001/01 1023/254/63 06 Fat16
	  6 x 002136645 004192965 1023/000/01 1023/254/63 05 extended
	  7 S 000000063 004192902 1023/001/01 1023/254/63 16 other
	  8 x 006329610 008401995 1023/000/01 1023/254/63 05 extended
	  9 S 000000063 008401932 1023/001/01 1023/254/63 0B Fat32
	 10 x 014731605 010490445 1023/000/01 1023/254/63 05 extended
	 11 S 000000063 010490382 1023/001/01 1023/254/63 83 Linux
	 12 x 025222050 004209030 1023/000/01 1023/254/63 05 extended
	 13 S 000000063 004208967 1023/001/01 1023/254/63 82 Linux swap
	 14 x 029431080 027712125 1023/000/01 1023/254/63 05 extended
	 15 S 000000063 027712062 1023/001/01 1023/254/63 07 NTFS
	 16 S 000000000 000000000 0000/000/00 0000/000/00 00 empty entry
	 17 P 000000000 000000000 0000/000/00 0000/000/00 00 empty entry
	 18 P 000000000 000000000 0000/000/00 0000/000/00 00 empty entry
	 1 020980827 sectors 10742183424 bytes
	 3 000032067 sectors 16418304 bytes
	 5 002104452 sectors 1077479424 bytes
	 7 004192902 sectors 2146765824 bytes
	 9 008401932 sectors 4301789184 bytes
	11 010490382 sectors 5371075584 bytes
	13 004208967 sectors 2154991104 bytes
	15 027712062 sectors 14188575744 bytes</pre>

Log Highlights:	====== Tool Settings ====== verify-hash off ====== Image file segments ====== 1 -rwx------ 1 ubuntu root 2136 2011-03-22 11:46 2011-03-22 11-

```
29-09 00003 D2F.LOG
     2 -rwx------ 1 ubuntu root 699990016 2011-03-22 11:29 IMAGE.001
     3 -rwx------ 1 ubuntu root 699990016 2011-03-22 11:29 IMAGE.002
    . . .
    57 -rwx------ 1 ubuntu root 699990016 2011-03-22 11:45 IMAGE.056
    58 -rwx------ 1 ubuntu root 699990016 2011-03-22 11:45 IMAGE.057
    59 -rwx------ 1 ubuntu root 100569088 2011-03-22 11:46 IMAGE.058

======== Excerpt from Log file ========
Task: Disk to File
Case:  DA-06-ATA28
# of sectors acquired: 78,125,000 (40.0 GB)
Chunk size in sectors: 1,367,168 (699.9 MB)
Chunks expected: 58
Chunks written: 58
Source hash:
 SHA1: 888e2e7f7ad237dc7a732281dd93f325065e5871
 MD5 : bc39c3f7ee7a50e77b9ba1e65a5aeef7

======== End of Excerpt from Log file ========

====== Source drive rehash ======
Rehash (SHA1) of source: 888E2E7F7AD237DC7A732281DD93F325065E5871
```

	Assertion & Expected Result	Actual Result
Results:	AM-01 Source acquired using interface AI.	as expected
	AM-02 Source is type DS.	as expected
	AM-03 Execution environment is XE.	as expected
	AM-05 An image is created on file system type FS.	as expected
	AM-06 All visible sectors acquired.	as expected
	AM-08 All sectors accurately acquired.	as expected
	AO-01 Image file is complete and accurate.	as expected
	AO-05 Multifile image created.	as expected
	AO-22 Tool calculates hashes by block.	option not available
	AO-23 Logged information is correct.	as expected
	AO-24 Source is unchanged by acquisition.	as expected
Analysis:	Expected results achieved	

5.2.8 DA-06-ATA48

Test Case DA-06-ATA48 Tableau TD1 Version 2.34	
Case Summary:	DA-06 Acquire a physical device using access interface AI to an image file.
Assertions:	AM-01 The tool uses access interface SRC-AI to access the digital source. AM-02 The tool acquires digital source DS. AM-03 The tool executes in execution environment XE. AM-05 If image file creation is specified, the tool creates an image file on file system type FS. AM-06 All visible sectors are acquired from the digital source. AM-08 All sectors acquired from the digital source are acquired accurately. AO-01 If the tool creates an image file, the data represented by the image file is the same as the data acquired by the tool. AO-05 If the tool creates a multi-file image of a requested size then all the individual files shall be no larger than the requested size. AO-22 If requested, the tool calculates block hashes for a specified block size during an acquisition for each block acquired from the digital source. AO-23 If the tool logs any log significant information, the information is accurately recorded in the log file. AO-24 If the tool executes in a forensically safe execution environment, the digital source is unchanged by the acquisition process.
Tester Name:	brl
Test Host:	TD1
Test Date:	Tue Mar 22 15:23:15 2011
Drives:	src(4C) dst (none) other (64-SATA)
Source Setup:	src hash (SHA1): < 8FF620D2BEDCCAFE8412EDAAD56C8554F872EFBF > src hash (MD5): < D10F763B56D4CEBA2D1311C61F9FB382 > 390721968 total sectors (200049647616 bytes) 24320/254/63 (max cyl/hd values) 24321/255/63 (number of cyl/hd) IDE disk: Model (WDC WD2000JB-00KFA0) serial # (WD-WMAMR1031111) N Start LBA Length Start C/H/S End C/H/S boot Partition type 1 P 000000063 390700737 0000/001/01 1023/254/63 Boot 07 NTFS 2 P 000000000 000000000 0000/000/00 0000/000/00 00 empty entry 3 P 000000000 000000000 0000/000/00 0000/000/00 00 empty entry 4 P 000000000 000000000 0000/000/00 0000/000/00 00 empty entry 1 390700737 sectors 200038777344 bytes

Log Highlights:	====== Tool Settings ======
	verify-hash off
	
	====== Image file segments ======
	    1 -rwx------ 1 ubuntu root 2150 2011-03-23 10:14 2011-03-23 09-
	06-35 00007 D2F.LOG
	    2 -rwx------ 1 ubuntu root 3999989760 2011-03-23 09:06 IMAGE.001
	    3 -rwx------ 1 ubuntu root 3999989760 2011-03-23 09:07 IMAGE.002
	    . . .
	   50 -rwx------ 1 ubuntu root 3999989760 2011-03-23 10:10 IMAGE.049
	   51 -rwx------ 1 ubuntu root 3999989760 2011-03-23 10:12 IMAGE.050
	   52 -rwx------ 1 ubuntu root 50159616 2011-03-23 10:14 IMAGE.051
	
	======== Excerpt from Log file ========
	Task: Disk to File
	Case: DA-06-ATA48
	# of sectors acquired: 390,721,968 (200.0 GB)
	Chunk size in sectors: 7,812,480 (3.9 GB)
	Chunks expected: 51
	Chunks written: 51
	Source hash:
	 SHA1: 8ff620d2bedccafe8412edaad56c8554f872efbf
	 MD5 : d10f763b56d4ceba2d1311c61f9fb382
	
	======== End of Excerpt from Log file ========
	
	====== Source drive rehash ======

Test Case DA-06-ATA48 Tableau TD1 Version 2.34	
	Rehash (SHA1) of source: 8FF620D2BEDCCAFE8412EDAAD56C8554F872EFBF

Results:	

Assertion & Expected Result	Actual Result
AM-01 Source acquired using interface AI.	as expected
AM-02 Source is type DS.	as expected
AM-03 Execution environment is XE.	as expected
AM-05 An image is created on file system type FS.	as expected
AM-06 All visible sectors acquired.	as expected
AM-08 All sectors accurately acquired.	as expected
AO-01 Image file is complete and accurate.	as expected
AO-05 Multifile image created.	as expected
AO-22 Tool calculates hashes by block.	option not available
AO-23 Logged information is correct.	as expected
AO-24 Source is unchanged by acquisition.	as expected

Analysis:	Expected results achieved

5.2.9 DA-06-ESATA

Test Case DA-06-ESATA Tableau TD1 Version 2.34	
Case Summary:	DA-06 Acquire a physical device using access interface AI to an image file.
Assertions:	AM-01 The tool uses access interface SRC-AI to access the digital source. AM-02 The tool acquires digital source DS. AM-03 The tool executes in execution environment XE. AM-05 If image file creation is specified, the tool creates an image file on file system type FS. AM-06 All visible sectors are acquired from the digital source. AM-08 All sectors acquired from the digital source are acquired accurately. AO-01 If the tool creates an image file, the data represented by the image file is the same as the data acquired by the tool. AO-05 If the tool creates a multi-file image of a requested size then all the individual files shall be no larger than the requested size. AO-22 If requested, the tool calculates block hashes for a specified block size during an acquisition for each block acquired from the digital source. AO-23 If the tool logs any log significant information, the information is accurately recorded in the log file. AO-24 If the tool executes in a forensically safe execution environment, the digital source is unchanged by the acquisition process.
Tester Name:	brl
Test Host:	TD1
Test Date:	Wed Mar 23 09:14:57 2011
Drives:	src(07-SATA) dst (none) other (64-SATA)
Source Setup:	src hash (SHA256): < CE65C4A3C3164D3EBAD58D33BB2415D29E260E1F88DC5A131B1C4C9C2945B8A9 > src hash (SHA1): < 655E9BDDB36A3F9C5C4CC8BF32B8C5B41AF9F52E > src hash (MD5): < 2EAF712DAD80F66E30DEA00365B4579B > 156301488 total sectors (80026361856 bytes) Model (WDC WD800JD-32HK) serial # (WD-WMAJ91510044) N Start LBA Length Start C/H/S End C/H/S boot Partition type 1 P 000000063 156280257 0000/001/01 1023/254/63 Boot 07 NTFS 2 P 000000000 000000000 0000/000/00 0000/000/00 00 empty entry 3 P 000000000 000000000 0000/000/00 0000/000/00 00 empty entry 4 P 000000000 000000000 0000/000/00 0000/000/00 00 empty entry 1 156280257 sectors 80015491584 bytes

Log Highlights:	====== Tool Settings ======
	verify-hash off
	
	====== Image file segments ======
	    1 -rwx------ 1 ubuntu root 2145 2011-03-23 11:11 2011-03-23 10-
	37-35 00008 D2F.LOG
	    2 -rwx------ 1 ubuntu root 999981056 2011-03-23 10:37 IMAGE.001
	    3 -rwx------ 1 ubuntu root 999981056 2011-03-23 10:38 IMAGE.002
	   . . .
	  80 -rwx------ 1 ubuntu root 999981056 2011-03-23 11:10 IMAGE.079
	  81 -rwx------ 1 ubuntu root 999981056 2011-03-23 11:10 IMAGE.080
	  82 -rwx------ 1 ubuntu root 27877376 2011-03-23 11:11 IMAGE.081
	
	======== Excerpt from Log file ========
	Task: Disk to File
	Case: DA-06-ESATA
	# of sectors acquired: 156,301,488 (80.0 GB)
	Chunk size in sectors: 1,953,088 (999.9 MB)
	Chunks expected: 81
	Chunks written: 81
	Source hash:
	 SHA1: 655e9bddb36a3f9c5c4cc8bf32b8c5b41af9f52e
	 MD5 : 2eaf712dad80f66e30dea00365b4579b
	
	======== End of Excerpt from Log file ========

Test Case DA-06-ESATA Tableau TD1 Version 2.34

	`====== Source drive rehash ======` `Rehash (SHA1) of source: 655E9BDDB36A3F9C5C4CC8BF32B8C5B41AF9F52E`
Results:	

Assertion & Expected Result	Actual Result
AM-01 Source acquired using interface AI.	as expected
AM-02 Source is type DS.	as expected
AM-03 Execution environment is XE.	as expected
AM-05 An image is created on file system type FS.	as expected
AM-06 All visible sectors acquired.	as expected
AM-08 All sectors accurately acquired.	as expected
AO-01 Image file is complete and accurate.	as expected
AO-05 Multifile image created.	as expected
AO-22 Tool calculates hashes by block.	option not available
AO-23 Logged information is correct.	as expected
AO-24 Source is unchanged by acquisition.	as expected

Analysis:	Expected results achieved

5.2.10   DA-06-SATA28

Test Case DA-06-SATA28 Tableau TD1 Version 2.34	
Case Summary:	DA-06 Acquire a physical device using access interface AI to an image file.
Assertions:	AM-01 The tool uses access interface SRC-AI to access the digital source. AM-02 The tool acquires digital source DS. AM-03 The tool executes in execution environment XE. AM-05 If image file creation is specified, the tool creates an image file on file system type FS. AM-06 All visible sectors are acquired from the digital source. AM-08 All sectors acquired from the digital source are acquired accurately. AO-01 If the tool creates an image file, the data represented by the image file is the same as the data acquired by the tool. AO-05 If the tool creates a multi-file image of a requested size then all the individual files shall be no larger than the requested size. AO-22 If requested, the tool calculates block hashes for a specified block size during an acquisition for each block acquired from the digital source. AO-23 If the tool logs any log significant information, the information is accurately recorded in the log file. AO-24 If the tool executes in a forensically safe execution environment, the digital source is unchanged by the acquisition process.
Tester Name:	brl
Test Host:	McGarrett
Test Date:	Fri Mar 25 08:58:58 2011
Drives:	src(07-SATA) dst (none) other (58-SATA)
Source Setup:	src hash (SHA256): < CE65C4A3C3164D3EBAD58D33BB2415D29E260E1F88DC5A131B1C4C9C2945B8A9 > src hash (SHA1): < 655E9BDDB36A3F9C5C4CC8BF32B8C5B41AF9F52E > src hash (MD5): < 2EAF712DAD80F66E30DEA00365B4579B > 156301488 total sectors (80026361856 bytes) Model (WDC WD800JD-32HK) serial # (WD-WMAJ91510044) N Start LBA Length Start C/H/S End C/H/S boot Partition type 1 P 000000063 156280257 0000/001/01 1023/254/63 Boot 07 NTFS 2 P 000000000 000000000 0000/000/00 0000/000/00 00 empty entry 3 P 000000000 000000000 0000/000/00 0000/000/00 00 empty entry 4 P 000000000 000000000 0000/000/00 0000/000/00 00 empty entry 1 156280257 sectors 80015491584 bytes

Log Highlights:	====== Tool Settings ======
	verify-hash off
	
	====== Image file segments ======
	    1 2163 2011-03-25 09:41 2011-0~1.log
	    2 999981056 2011-03-25 09:08 image.001
	    3 999981056 2011-03-25 09:08 image.002
	  . . .
	   80 999981056 2011-03-25 09:40 image.079
	   81 999981056 2011-03-25 09:41 image.080
	   82 27877376 2011-03-25 09:41 image.081
	
	======== Excerpt from Log file ========
	Task: Disk to File
	Case: DA-06-SATA28
	# of sectors acquired: 156,301,488 (80.0 GB)
	Chunk size in sectors: 1,953,088 (999.9 MB)
	Chunks expected: 81
	Chunks written: 81
	Source hash:
	 SHA1: 655e9bddb36a3f9c5c4cc8bf32b8c5b41af9f52e
	 MD5 : 2eaf712dad80f66e30dea00365b4579b
	
	======== End of Excerpt from Log file ========
	
	====== Source drive rehash ======

Test Case DA-06-SATA28 Tableau TD1 Version 2.34	
	Rehash (SHA1) of source: 655E9BDDB36A3F9C5C4CC8BF32B8C5B41AF9F52E
Results:	

Assertion & Expected Result	Actual Result
AM-01 Source acquired using interface AI.	as expected
AM-02 Source is type DS.	as expected
AM-03 Execution environment is XE.	as expected
AM-05 An image is created on file system type FS.	as expected
AM-06 All visible sectors acquired.	as expected
AM-08 All sectors accurately acquired.	as expected
AO-01 Image file is complete and accurate.	as expected
AO-05 Multifile image created.	as expected
AO-22 Tool calculates hashes by block.	option not available
AO-23 Logged information is correct.	as expected
AO-24 Source is unchanged by acquisition.	as expected

Analysis:	Expected results achieved

5.2.11   DA-06-SATA48

Test Case DA-06-SATA48 Tableau TD1 Version 2.34	
Case Summary:	DA-06 Acquire a physical device using access interface AI to an image file.
Assertions:	AM-01 The tool uses access interface SRC-AI to access the digital source. AM-02 The tool acquires digital source DS. AM-03 The tool executes in execution environment XE. AM-05 If image file creation is specified, the tool creates an image file on file system type FS. AM-06 All visible sectors are acquired from the digital source. AM-08 All sectors acquired from the digital source are acquired accurately. AO-01 If the tool creates an image file, the data represented by the image file is the same as the data acquired by the tool. AO-05 If the tool creates a multi-file image of a requested size then all the individual files shall be no larger than the requested size. AO-22 If requested, the tool calculates block hashes for a specified block size during an acquisition for each block acquired from the digital source. AO-23 If the tool logs any log significant information, the information is accurately recorded in the log file. AO-24 If the tool executes in a forensically safe execution environment, the digital source is unchanged by the acquisition process.
Tester Name:	brl
Test Host:	TD1
Test Date:	Tue Mar 22 15:59:37 2011
Drives:	src(0D-SATA) dst (none) other (39-SATA)
Source Setup:	src hash (SHA1): < BAAD80E8781E55F2E3EF528CA73BD41D228C1377 > src hash (MD5): < 1FA7C3CBE60EB9E89863DED2411E40C9 > 488397168 total sectors (250059350016 bytes) 30400/254/63 (max cyl/hd values) 30401/255/63 (number of cyl/hd) Model (WDC WD2500JD-22F) serial # (WD-WMAEH2678216) N Start LBA Length Start C/H/S End C/H/S boot Partition type 1 P 000000063 488375937 0000/001/01 1023/254/63 Boot 07 NTFS 2 P 000000000 000000000 0000/000/00 0000/000/00 00 empty entry 3 P 000000000 000000000 0000/000/00 0000/000/00 00 empty entry 4 P 000000000 000000000 0000/000/00 0000/000/00 00 empty entry 1 488375937 sectors 250048479744 bytes

Log Highlights:	====== Tool Settings ======
	verify-hash on
	
	====== Image file segments ======
	    1 -rwx------ 1 ubuntu root 2272 2011-03-23 12:15 2011-03-23 09-30-53 00010 D2F.LOG
	    2 -rwx------ 1 ubuntu root 3999989760 2011-03-23 09:30 IMAGE.001
	    3 -rwx------ 1 ubuntu root 3999989760 2011-03-23 09:32 IMAGE.002
	  . . .
	    62 -rwx------ 1 ubuntu root 3999989760 2011-03-23 11:02 IMAGE.061
	    63 -rwx------ 1 ubuntu root 3999989760 2011-03-23 11:04 IMAGE.062
	    64 -rwx------ 1 ubuntu root 2059984896 2011-03-23 11:06 IMAGE.063
	
	======== Excerpt from Log file ========
	Task: Disk to File
	Case: DA-06-SATA48
	# of sectors acquired: 488,397,168 (250.0 GB)
	Chunk size in sectors: 7,812,480 (3.9 GB)
	Chunks expected: 63
	Chunks written: 63
	Source hash:
	 SHA1: baad80e8781e55f2e3ef528ca73bd41d228c1377
	 MD5 : 1fa7c3cbe60eb9e89863ded2411e40c9
	Verification hash:
	 SHA1: baad80e8781e55f2e3ef528ca73bd41d228c1377
	 MD5 : 1fa7c3cbe60eb9e89863ded2411e40c9

Test Case DA-06-SATA48 Tableau TD1 Version 2.34	
	======== End of Excerpt from Log file ======== ====== Source drive rehash ====== Rehash (SHA1) of source: BAAD80E8781E55F2E3EF528CA73BD41D228C1377
Results:	

Assertion & Expected Result	Actual Result
AM-01 Source acquired using interface AI.	as expected
AM-02 Source is type DS.	as expected
AM-03 Execution environment is XE.	as expected
AM-05 An image is created on file system type FS.	as expected
AM-06 All visible sectors acquired.	as expected
AM-08 All sectors accurately acquired.	as expected
AO-01 Image file is complete and accurate.	as expected
AO-05 Multifile image created.	as expected
AO-22 Tool calculates hashes by block.	option not available
AO-23 Logged information is correct.	as expected
AO-24 Source is unchanged by acquisition.	as expected

Analysis:	Expected results achieved

5.2.12   DA-08-ATA28

Test Case DA-08-ATA28 Tableau TD1 Version 2.34	
Case Summary:	DA-08 Acquire a physical drive with hidden sectors to an image file.
Assertions:	AM-01 The tool uses access interface SRC-AI to access the digital source. AM-02 The tool acquires digital source DS. AM-03 The tool executes in execution environment XE. AM-05 If image file creation is specified, the tool creates an image file on file system type FS. AM-06 All visible sectors are acquired from the digital source. AM-07 All hidden sectors are acquired from the digital source. AM-08 All sectors acquired from the digital source are acquired accurately. AO-01 If the tool creates an image file, the data represented by the image file is the same as the data acquired by the tool. AO-05 If the tool creates a multi-file image of a requested size then all the individual files shall be no larger than the requested size. AO-22 If requested, the tool calculates block hashes for a specified block size during an acquisition for each block acquired from the digital source. AO-23 If the tool logs any log significant information, the information is accurately recorded in the log file. AO-24 If the tool executes in a forensically safe execution environment, the digital source is unchanged by the acquisition process.
Tester Name:	brl
Test Host:	TD1
Test Date:	Thu Mar 24 12:50:53 2011
Drives:	src(42) dst (none) other (39-SATA)
Source Setup:	src hash (SHA1): < 5A75399023056E0EB905082B35F8FAA1DB049229 > src hash (MD5): < F4B9AAB24554EEEB2A962BDA554A9252 > 78165360 total sectors (40020664320 bytes) 65534/015/63 (max cyl/hd values) 65535/016/63 (number of cyl/hd) IDE disk: Model (WDC WD400JB-00JJC0) serial # (WD-WCAMA3958512) N Start LBA Length Start C/H/S End C/H/S boot Partition type 1 P 000000063 070348572 0000/001/01 1023/254/63 Boot 07 NTFS 2 P 000000000 000000000 0000/000/00 0000/000/00 00 empty entry 3 P 000000000 000000000 0000/000/00 0000/000/00 00 empty entry 4 P 000000000 000000000 0000/000/00 0000/000/00 00 empty entry 1 070348572 sectors 36018468864 bytes HPA created BIOS, XBIOS and Direct disk geometry Reporter (BXDR) BXDR 128 /S70000000 /P /fbxdrlog.txt Setting Maximum Addressable Sector to 70000000 MAS now set to 70000000 Hashes with HPA in place md5:9BF3C3DEADE47056A1DDC073C5F6B2E2 sha1:D76F909482B00767B62C295CADE202F92E61CD2E

Log Highlights:	====== Tool Message ======
	ALERT
	Source disk may be blank.
	
	====== Tool Settings ======
	verify-hash off
	
	====== Image file segments ======
	    1 -rwx------ 1 ubuntu root 2146 2011-03-24 13:26 2011-03-24 13-10-08 00015 D2F.LOG
	    2 -rwx------ 1 ubuntu root 3999989760 2011-03-24 13:10 IMAGE.001
	    3 -rwx------ 1 ubuntu root 3999989760 2011-03-24 13:11 IMAGE.002
	  . . .
	   10 -rwx------ 1 ubuntu root 3999989760 2011-03-24 13:22 IMAGE.009
	   11 -rwx------ 1 ubuntu root 3999989760 2011-03-24 13:24 IMAGE.010
	   12 -rwx------ 1 ubuntu root 20766720 2011-03-24 13:26 IMAGE.011

```
======== Excerpt from Log file ========
Task: Disk to File
Case:   DA-08-ATA28
# of sectors acquired: 78,165,360 (40.0 GB)
Chunk size in sectors: 7,812,480 (3.9 GB)
Chunks expected: 11
Chunks written: 11

Model: WDC WD400JB-00JJC0
S/N: WD-WCAMA3958512
Firmware Revision: 05.01C05
Capacity in sectors reported Pwr-ON: 70,000,001 (35.8 GB)
Capacity in sectors reported by HPA: 78,165,360 (40.0 GB)
Capacity in sectors reported by DCO: 78,165,360 (40.0 GB)
HPA in use: Yes
DCO in use: No
ATA Security in use: No
Cable/Interface type: IDE
Source hash:
 SHA1: 5a75399023056e0eb905082b35f8faa1db049229
 MD5 : f4b9aab24554eeeb2a962bda554a9252

======== End of Excerpt from Log file ========

====== Source drive rehash ======
Rehash (SHA1) of source: 5A75399023056E0EB905082B35F8FAA1DB049229
```

Results:	

Assertion & Expected Result	Actual Result
AM-01 Source acquired using interface AI.	as expected
AM-02 Source is type DS.	as expected
AM-03 Execution environment is XE.	as expected
AM-05 An image is created on file system type FS.	as expected
AM-06 All visible sectors acquired.	as expected
AM-07 All hidden sectors acquired.	as expected
AM-08 All sectors accurately acquired.	as expected
AO-01 Image file is complete and accurate.	as expected
AO-05 Multifile image created.	as expected
AO-22 Tool calculates hashes by block.	option not available
AO-23 Logged information is correct.	bogus error message
AO-24 Source is unchanged by acquisition.	as expected

Analysis:	Expected results not achieved

5.2.13　　DA-08-DCO

Test Case DA-08-DCO Tableau TD1 Version 2.34	
Case Summary:	DA-08 Acquire a physical drive with hidden sectors to an image file.
Assertions:	AM-01 The tool uses access interface SRC-AI to access the digital source. AM-02 The tool acquires digital source DS. AM-03 The tool executes in execution environment XE. AM-05 If image file creation is specified, the tool creates an image file on file system type FS. AM-06 All visible sectors are acquired from the digital source. AM-07 All hidden sectors are acquired from the digital source. AM-08 All sectors acquired from the digital source are acquired accurately. AO-01 If the tool creates an image file, the data represented by the image file is the same as the data acquired by the tool. AO-05 If the tool creates a multi-file image of a requested size then all the individual files shall be no larger than the requested size. AO-22 If requested, the tool calculates block hashes for a specified block size during an acquisition for each block acquired from the digital source. AO-23 If the tool logs any log significant information, the information is accurately recorded in the log file. AO-24 If the tool executes in a forensically safe execution environment, the digital source is unchanged by the acquisition process.
Tester Name:	brl
Test Host:	TD1
Test Date:	Thu Mar 24 14:30:04 2011
Drives:	src(15-SATA) dst (none) other (39-SATA)
Source Setup:	src hash (SHA1): < 76B22DDE84CE61F090791DDBB79057529AAF00E1 > src hash (MD5): < 9B4A9D124107819A9CE6F253FE7DC675 > 156301488 total sectors (80026361856 bytes) Model (0JD-00HKA0　　　　) serial # (WD-WMAJ91513490) DCO Created with Maximum LBA Sectors = 140,000,000 Hashes with DCO in place: md5: E5F8B277A39ED0F49794E9916CD62DD9 sha1: AC64CF1B3736BB2FE40C14D871E6F207BC432C2F
Log Highlights:	====== Tool Message ====== **ALERT** Source disk DCO has not been removed. ====== Tool Settings ====== verify-hash off ====== Image file segments ====== 　　　1 -rwx------ 1 ubuntu root　　　　2146 2011-03-24 15:03 2011-03-24 14-34-45 00016 D2F.LOG 　　　　2 -rwx------ 1 ubuntu root 3999989760 2011-03-24 14:34 IMAGE.001 　　　　3 -rwx------ 1 ubuntu root 3999989760 2011-03-24 14:36 IMAGE.002 　　. . . 　　17 -rwx------ 1 ubuntu root 3999989760 2011-03-24 14:58 IMAGE.016 　　18 -rwx------ 1 ubuntu root 3999989760 2011-03-24 15:00 IMAGE.017 　　19 -rwx------ 1 ubuntu root 3680174592 2011-03-24 15:02 IMAGE.018 ======== Excerpt from Log file ======== Task: Disk to File Case:　 DA-08-DCO # of sectors acquired: 140,000,001 (71.6 GB) Chunk size in sectors: 7,812,480 (3.9 GB) Chunks expected: 18 Chunks written: 18 Model: WDC WD800JD-00HKA0 S/N: WD-WMAJ91513490 Firmware Revision: 13.03G13 Capacity in sectors reported Pwr-ON: 140,000,001 (71.6 GB)

Test Case DA-08-DCO Tableau TD1 Version 2.34	
	Capacity in sectors reported by HPA: 140,000,001 (71.6 GB) Capacity in sectors reported by DCO: 156,301,488 (80.0 GB) HPA in use: No DCO in use: Yes ATA Security in use: No Cable/Interface type: SATA Source hash: SHA1: ac64cf1b3736bb2fe40c14d871e6f207bc432c2f MD5 : e5f8b277a39ed0f49794e9916cd62dd9 ======== End of Excerpt from Log file ======== ====== Source drive rehash ====== Rehash (SHA1) of source: AC64CF1B3736BB2FE40C14D871E6F207BC432C2F
Results:	

Assertion & Expected Result	Actual Result
AM-01 Source acquired using interface AI.	as expected
AM-02 Source is type DS.	as expected
AM-03 Execution environment is XE.	as expected
AM-05 An image is created on file system type FS.	as expected
AM-06 All visible sectors acquired.	as expected
AM-07 All hidden sectors acquired.	DCO not acquired
AM-08 All sectors accurately acquired.	as expected
AO-01 Image file is complete and accurate.	as expected
AO-05 Multifile image created.	as expected
AO-22 Tool calculates hashes by block.	option not available
AO-23 Logged information is correct.	as expected
AO-24 Source is unchanged by acquisition.	as expected

Analysis:	Expected results not achieved

5.2.14   DA-08-DCO-ALT

Test Case DA-08-DCO-ALT Tableau TD1 Version 2.34	
Case Summary:	DA-08 Acquire a physical drive with hidden sectors to an image file.
Assertions:	AM-01 The tool uses access interface SRC-AI to access the digital source. AM-02 The tool acquires digital source DS. AM-03 The tool executes in execution environment XE. AM-05 If image file creation is specified, the tool creates an image file on file system type FS. AM-06 All visible sectors are acquired from the digital source. AM-07 All hidden sectors are acquired from the digital source. AM-08 All sectors acquired from the digital source are acquired accurately. AO-01 If the tool creates an image file, the data represented by the image file is the same as the data acquired by the tool. AO-05 If the tool creates a multi-file image of a requested size then all the individual files shall be no larger than the requested size. AO-22 If requested, the tool calculates block hashes for a specified block size during an acquisition for each block acquired from the digital source. AO-23 If the tool logs any log significant information, the information is accurately recorded in the log file. AO-24 If the tool executes in a forensically safe execution environment, the digital source is unchanged by the acquisition process.
Tester Name:	brl
Test Host:	TD1
Test Date:	Thu Mar 24 15:04:36 2011
Drives:	src(92) dst (none) other (39-SATA)

Source Setup:	src hash (SHA1): < 63E6F7BD3040A8ADA2CF8FBF66A805B76DF10481 >
	src hash (MD5): < E095DD1BD0B0DD6E603153A3FE1A2F3E >
	58633344 total sectors (30020272128 bytes)
	58167/015/63 (max cyl/hd values)
	58168/016/63 (number of cyl/hd)
	IDE disk: Model (WDC WD300BB-00CAA0) serial # (WD-WMA8H2140350)
	  N Start LBA Length Start C/H/S End C/H/S boot Partition type
	  1 P 000000063 058605057 0000/001/01 1023/254/63 Boot 07 NTFS
	  2 P 000000000 000000000 0000/000/00 0000/000/00 00 empty entry
	  3 P 000000000 000000000 0000/000/00 0000/000/00 00 empty entry
	  4 P 000000000 000000000 0000/000/00 0000/000/00 00 empty entry
	  1 058605057 sectors 30005789184 bytes
	
	Hashes with DCO in place:
	md5:525963C6789423396FE1F3202A8CBD04
	sha1:55A3CFE756B7B0034DCCE71F7D7A477D8681B781

Log Highlights:	====== Tool Message ======
	ALERT
	Source disk may be blank.
	
	====== Tool Settings ======
	verify-hash off
	
	====== Image file segments ======
	    1 -rwx------ 1 ubuntu root 2147 2011-03-24 16:12 2011-03-24 15-58-39 00017 D2F.LOG
	    2 -rwx------ 1 ubuntu root 3999989760 2011-03-24 15:58 IMAGE.001
	    3 -rwx------ 1 ubuntu root 3999989760 2011-03-24 16:00 IMAGE.002
	   . . .
	    6 -rwx------ 1 ubuntu root 3999989760 2011-03-24 16:06 IMAGE.005
	    7 -rwx------ 1 ubuntu root 3999989760 2011-03-24 16:08 IMAGE.006
	    8 -rwx------ 1 ubuntu root 3018306560 2011-03-24 16:10 IMAGE.007
	
	======= Excerpt from Log file =======
	Task: Disk to File
	Case: DA-08-DCO-ALT
	# of sectors acquired: 52,770,010 (27.0 GB)
	Chunk size in sectors: 7,812,480 (3.9 GB)

```
                    Chunks expected: 7
                    Chunks written: 7

                    Model: WDC WD300BB-00CAA0
                    S/N: WD-WMA8H2140350
                    Firmware Revision: 16.06V16
                    Capacity in sectors reported Pwr-ON: 52,770,010 (27.0 GB)
                    Capacity in sectors reported by HPA: 52,770,010 (27.0 GB)
                    Capacity in sectors reported by DCO: 58,633,344 (30.0 GB)
                    HPA in use: No
                    DCO in use: Yes
                    ATA Security in use: No
                    Cable/Interface type: IDE
                    Source hash:
                     SHA1: 55a3cfe756b7b0034dcce71f7d7a477d8681b781
                     MD5 : 525963c6789423396fe1f3202a8cbd04


                    ======== End of Excerpt from Log file ========

                    ====== Source drive rehash ======
                    Rehash (SHA1) of source: 55A3CFE756B7B0034DCCE71F7D7A477D8681B781
```

Results:		
	Assertion & Expected Result	**Actual Result**
	AM-01 Source acquired using interface AI.	as expected
	AM-02 Source is type DS.	as expected
	AM-03 Execution environment is XE.	as expected
	AM-05 An image is created on file system type FS.	as expected
	AM-06 All visible sectors acquired.	as expected
	AM-07 All hidden sectors acquired.	DCO not acquired
	AM-08 All sectors accurately acquired.	as expected
	AO-01 Image file is complete and accurate.	as expected
	AO-05 Multifile image created.	as expected
	AO-22 Tool calculates hashes by block.	option not available
	AO-23 Logged information is correct.	bogus error message
	AO-24 Source is unchanged by acquisition.	as expected
Analysis:	Expected results not achieved	

5.2.15   DA-08-DCO-ALT-SATA

Test Case DA-08-DCO-ALT-SATA Tableau TD1 Version 2.34	
Case Summary:	DA-08 Acquire a physical drive with hidden sectors to an image file.
Assertions:	AM-01 The tool uses access interface SRC-AI to access the digital source. AM-02 The tool acquires digital source DS. AM-03 The tool executes in execution environment XE. AM-05 If image file creation is specified, the tool creates an image file on file system type FS. AM-06 All visible sectors are acquired from the digital source. AM-07 All hidden sectors are acquired from the digital source. AM-08 All sectors acquired from the digital source are acquired accurately. AO-01 If the tool creates an image file, the data represented by the image file is the same as the data acquired by the tool. AO-05 If the tool creates a multi-file image of a requested size then all the individual files shall be no larger than the requested size. AO-22 If requested, the tool calculates block hashes for a specified block size during an acquisition for each block acquired from the digital source. AO-23 If the tool logs any log significant information, the information is accurately recorded in the log file. AO-24 If the tool executes in a forensically safe execution environment, the digital source is unchanged by the acquisition process.
Tester Name:	brl
Test Host:	TD1
Test Date:	Mon Mar 28 09:25:04 2011
Drives:	src(15-SATA) dst (none) other (39-SATA)
Source Setup:	src hash (SHA1): < 76B22DDE84CE61F090791DDBB79057529AAF00E1 > src hash (MD5): < 9B4A9D124107819A9CE6F253FE7DC675 > 156301488 total sectors (80026361856 bytes) Model (0JD-00HKA0) serial # (WD-WMAJ91513490) DCO Created with Maximum LBA Sectors = 140,000,000 Hashes with DCO in place: md5: E5F8B277A39ED0F49794E9916CD62DD9 sha1: AC64CF1B3736BB2FE40C14D871E6F207BC432C2F

Log Highlights:	====== Tool Message ======
	ALERT
	Source disk DCO has not been removed.
	
	====== Tool Settings ======
	verify-hash off
	
	====== Image file segments ======
	    1 -rwx------ 1 ubuntu root 2163 2011-03-28 10:29 2011-03-28 09-56-11 00019 D2F.LOG
	     2 -rwx------ 1 ubuntu root 3999989760 2011-03-28 09:56 IMAGE.001
	     3 -rwx------ 1 ubuntu root 3999989760 2011-03-28 09:57 IMAGE.002
	  . . .
	   20 -rwx------ 1 ubuntu root 3999989760 2011-03-28 10:25 IMAGE.019
	   21 -rwx------ 1 ubuntu root 3999989760 2011-03-28 10:27 IMAGE.020
	   22 -rwx------ 1 ubuntu root 26566656 2011-03-28 10:29 IMAGE.021
	
	======== Excerpt from Log file ========
	Task: Disk to File
	Case: DA-08-DCO-ALT-SATA
	# of sectors acquired: 156,301,488 (80.0 GB)
	Chunk size in sectors: 7,812,480 (3.9 GB)
	Chunks expected: 21
	Chunks written: 21
	
	Model: WDC WD800JD-00HKA0
	S/N: WD-WMAJ91513490
	Firmware Revision: 13.03G13
	Capacity in sectors reported Pwr-ON: 156,301,488 (80.0 GB)

	Capacity in sectors reported by HPA: 156,301,488 (80.0 GB) Capacity in sectors reported by DCO: 156,301,488 (80.0 GB) HPA in use: No DCO in use: No ATA Security in use: No Cable/Interface type: SATA Source hash: SHA1: 76b22dde84ce61f090791ddbb79057529aaf00e1 MD5 : 9b4a9d124107819a9ce6f253fe7dc675 ======== End of Excerpt from Log file ======== ====== Source drive rehash ====== Rehash (SHA1) of source: 76B22DDE84CE61F090791DDBB79057529AAF00E1
Results:	

Assertion & Expected Result	Actual Result
AM-01 Source acquired using interface AI.	as expected
AM-02 Source is type DS.	as expected
AM-03 Execution environment is XE.	as expected
AM-05 An image is created on file system type FS.	as expected
AM-06 All visible sectors acquired.	as expected
AM-07 All hidden sectors acquired.	as expected
AM-08 All sectors accurately acquired.	as expected
AO-01 Image file is complete and accurate.	as expected
AO-05 Multifile image created.	as expected
AO-22 Tool calculates hashes by block.	option not available
AO-23 Logged information is correct.	as expected
AO-24 Source is unchanged by acquisition.	as expected

Analysis:	Expected results achieved

5.2.16 DA-08-SATA48

Test Case DA-08-SATA48 Tableau TD1 Version 2.34	
Case Summary:	DA-08 Acquire a physical drive with hidden sectors to an image file.
Assertions:	AM-01 The tool uses access interface SRC-AI to access the digital source. AM-02 The tool acquires digital source DS. AM-03 The tool executes in execution environment XE. AM-05 If image file creation is specified, the tool creates an image file on file system type FS. AM-06 All visible sectors are acquired from the digital source. AM-07 All hidden sectors are acquired from the digital source. AM-08 All sectors acquired from the digital source are acquired accurately. AO-01 If the tool creates an image file, the data represented by the image file is the same as the data acquired by the tool. AO-05 If the tool creates a multi-file image of a requested size then all the individual files shall be no larger than the requested size. AO-22 If requested, the tool calculates block hashes for a specified block size during an acquisition for each block acquired from the digital source. AO-23 If the tool logs any log significant information, the information is accurately recorded in the log file. AO-24 If the tool executes in a forensically safe execution environment, the digital source is unchanged by the acquisition process.
Tester Name:	brl
Test Host:	TD1
Test Date:	Thu Mar 24 13:17:25 2011
Drives:	src(1E-SATA) dst (none) other (64-SATA)
Source Setup:	src hash (SHA1): < 3E7439D9E99ACD030B969C1BE5B1430BF7183573 > src hash (MD5): < 8E1CF5E20E86362E0EACF12EDDEF42A6 > 625142448 total sectors (320072933376 bytes) 38912/254/63 (max cyl/hd values) 38913/255/63 (number of cyl/hd) Model (ST3320620AS) serial # (5QF3X4F6) HPA created HPA Created with Maximum LBA Sectors = 560,000,000 Hashes with HPA in place md5: 3655FA5086B6864154898533DFAE2442 sha1: EB1045B57DE7CDA28FE9504E3FA238D0B5DBC587

Log Highlights:	====== Tool Message ======
	ALERT
	Source disk HPA has been auto removed.
	
	====== Tool Settings ======
	verify-hash off
	
	====== Image file segments ======
	   1 -rwx------ 1 ubuntu root 2137 2011-03-24 15:12 2011-03-24 13-47-49 00010 D2F.LOG
	   2 -rwx------ 1 ubuntu root 3999989760 2011-03-24 13:47 IMAGE.001
	   3 -rwx------ 1 ubuntu root 3999989760 2011-03-24 13:48 IMAGE.002
	   . . .
	  80 -rwx------ 1 ubuntu root 3999989760 2011-03-24 15:09 IMAGE.079
	  81 -rwx------ 1 ubuntu root 3999989760 2011-03-24 15:10 IMAGE.080
	  82 -rwx------ 1 ubuntu root 73752576 2011-03-24 15:12 IMAGE.081
	
	======== Excerpt from Log file ========
	Task: Disk to File
	Case: DA-08-SATA48
	# of sectors acquired: 625,142,448 (320.0 GB)
	Chunk size in sectors: 7,812,480 (3.9 GB)
	Chunks expected: 81
	Chunks written: 81

Test Case DA-08-SATA48 Tableau TD1 Version 2.34	
	Model: ST3320620AS S/N: 5QF3X4F6 Firmware Revision: 3.AAK Capacity in sectors reported Pwr-ON: 560,000,001 (286.7 GB) Capacity in sectors reported by HPA: 625,142,448 (320.0 GB) Capacity in sectors reported by DCO: 625,142,448 (320.0 GB) HPA in use: Yes DCO in use: No ATA Security in use: No Cable/Interface type: SATA Source hash: SHA1: 3e7439d9e99acd030b969c1be5b1430bf7183573 MD5 : 8e1cf5e20e86362e0eacf12eddef42a6 ======== End of Excerpt from Log file ======== ====== Source drive rehash ====== Rehash (SHA1) of source: 3E7439D9E99ACD030B969C1BE5B1430BF7183573
Results:	

Assertion & Expected Result	Actual Result
AM-01 Source acquired using interface AI.	as expected
AM-02 Source is type DS.	as expected
AM-03 Execution environment is XE.	as expected
AM-05 An image is created on file system type FS.	as expected
AM-06 All visible sectors acquired.	as expected
AM-07 All hidden sectors acquired.	as expected
AM-08 All sectors accurately acquired.	as expected
AO-01 Image file is complete and accurate.	as expected
AO-05 Multifile image created.	as expected
AO-22 Tool calculates hashes by block.	option not available
AO-23 Logged information is correct.	as expected
AO-24 Source is unchanged by acquisition.	as expected

Analysis:	Expected results achieved

5.2.17 DA-09-COMPLETE

Test Case DA-09-COMPLETE Tableau TD1 Version 2.34	
Case Summary:	DA-09 Acquire a digital source that has at least one faulty data sector.
Assertions:	AM-01 The tool uses access interface SRC-AI to access the digital source. AM-02 The tool acquires digital source DS. AM-03 The tool executes in execution environment XE. AM-05 If image file creation is specified, the tool creates an image file on file system type FS. AM-06 All visible sectors are acquired from the digital source. AM-08 All sectors acquired from the digital source are acquired accurately. AM-09 If unresolved errors occur while reading from the selected digital source, the tool notifies the user of the error type and location within the digital source. AM-10 If unresolved errors occur while reading from the selected digital source, the tool uses a benign fill in the destination object in place of the inaccessible data. AO-01 If the tool creates an image file, the data represented by the image file is the same as the data acquired by the tool. AO-05 If the tool creates a multi-file image of a requested size then all the individual files shall be no larger than the requested size. AO-22 If requested, the tool calculates block hashes for a specified block size during an acquisition for each block acquired from the digital source. AO-23 If the tool logs any log significant information, the information is accurately recorded in the log file. AO-24 If the tool executes in a forensically safe execution environment, the digital source is unchanged by the acquisition process.
Tester Name:	brl
Test Host:	TD1
Test Date:	Fri Mar 25 10:32:34 2011
Drives:	src(ED-BAD-CPR4) dst (none) other (78-SATA-SSD)
Source Setup:	No before hash for ED-BAD-CPR4 Known Bad Sector List for ED-BAD-CPR4 Manufacturer: Maxtor Model: DiamondMax Plus 9 Serial Number: Y23EGSJE Capacity: 60GB Interface: SATA 35 faulty sectors 6160328, 6160362, 10041157, 10041995, 10118634, 10209448, 11256569, 14115689, 14778391, 14778392, 14778449, 14778479, 14778517, 14778518, 14778519, 14778520, 14778521, 14778551, 14778607, 14778626, 14778627, 14778650, 14778668, 14778669, 14778709, 14778727, 14778747, 14778772, 14778781, 14778870, 14778949, 14778953, 14779038, 14779113, 14779321
Log Highlights:	====== Destination drive setup ====== 125045424 sectors wiped with 78 ====== Comparison of original to clone drive ====== Sectors compared: 120103200 Sectors match: 120103165 Sectors differ: 35 Bytes differ: 17885 Diffs range 6160328, 6160362, 10041157, 10041995, 10118634, 10209448, 11256569, 14115689, 14778391-14778392, 14778449, 14778479, 14778517-14778521, 14778551, 14778607, 14778626-14778627, 14778650, 14778668-14778669, 14778709, 14778727, 14778747, 14778772, 14778781, 14778870, 14778949, 14778953, 14779038, 14779113, 14779321 Source (120103200) has 4942224 fewer sectors than destination (125045424) Zero fill: 0 Src Byte fill (ED): 0

```
                    Dst Byte fill (78):  4942224
                    Other fill:                0
                    Other no fill:             0
                    Zero fill range:
                    Src fill range:
                    Dst fill range:  120103200-125045423
                    Other fill range:
                    Other not filled range:
                    0 source read errors, 0 destination read errors


                    ====== Tool Settings ======
                    error-recovery complete


                    ======== Excerpt from Log file ========
                    Task: Disk to Disk
                    Case:  DA-09-COMPLETE
                    # of sectors acquired: 120,103,200 (61.4 GB)
                    Total errors: 28
                    Errors recorded: 28
                    -----------------------List of errors-----------------------
                    Error # 1: Read error (source), address=6160328, length=1
                    Error # 2: Read error (source), address=6160362, length=1
                    Error # 3: Read error (source), address=10041157, length=1
                    Error # 4: Read error (source), address=10041995, length=1
                    Error # 5: Read error (source), address=10118634, length=1
                      . . .
                    Error # 24: Read error (source), address=14778949, length=1
                    Error # 25: Read error (source), address=14778953, length=1
                    Error # 26: Read error (source), address=14779038, length=1
                    Error # 27: Read error (source), address=14779113, length=1
                    Error # 28: Read error (source), address=14779321, length=1
                    ======== End of Excerpt from Log file ========
```

Results:		
	Assertion & Expected Result	**Actual Result**
	AM-01 Source acquired using interface AI.	as expected
	AM-02 Source is type DS.	as expected
	AM-03 Execution environment is XE.	as expected
	AM-05 An image is created on file system type FS.	as expected
	AM-06 All visible sectors acquired.	as expected
	AM-08 All sectors accurately acquired.	as expected
	AM-09 Error logged.	as expected
	AM-10 Benign fill replaces inaccessible sectors.	as expected
	AO-01 Image file is complete and accurate.	as expected
	AO-05 Multifile image created.	as expected
	AO-22 Tool calculates hashes by block.	option not available
	AO-23 Logged information is correct.	as expected
	AO-24 Source is unchanged by acquisition.	not checked

Analysis:	Expected results achieved

5.2.18   DA-09-FAST

Test Case DA-09-FAST Tableau TD1 Version 2.34	
Case Summary:	DA-09 Acquire a digital source that has at least one faulty data sector.
Assertions:	AM-01 The tool uses access interface SRC-AI to access the digital source. AM-02 The tool acquires digital source DS. AM-03 The tool executes in execution environment XE. AM-05 If image file creation is specified, the tool creates an image file on file system type FS. AM-06 All visible sectors are acquired from the digital source. AM-08 All sectors acquired from the digital source are acquired accurately. AM-09 If unresolved errors occur while reading from the selected digital source, the tool notifies the user of the error type and location within the digital source. AM-10 If unresolved errors occur while reading from the selected digital source, the tool uses a benign fill in the destination object in place of the inaccessible data. AO-01 If the tool creates an image file, the data represented by the image file is the same as the data acquired by the tool. AO-05 If the tool creates a multi-file image of a requested size then all the individual files shall be no larger than the requested size. AO-22 If requested, the tool calculates block hashes for a specified block size during an acquisition for each block acquired from the digital source. AO-23 If the tool logs any log significant information, the information is accurately recorded in the log file. AO-24 If the tool executes in a forensically safe execution environment, the digital source is unchanged by the acquisition process.
Tester Name:	brl
Test Host:	TD1
Test Date:	Fri Mar 25 09:25:38 2011
Drives:	src(ED-BAD-CPR3) dst (79-SATA-SSD) other (none)
Source Setup:	No before hash for ED-BAD-CPR3 Known Bad Sector List for ED-CPR-BAD-3 Manufacturer: Maxtor Model: DiamondMax Plus 9 Serial Number: Y239EQSE Capacity: 60GB Interface: PATA 398 bad sectors 67407, 68223, 688162, 1769014, 1772576, 2215215, 2215216, 2664136, 3155361, 3155362, 4768530, 4768531, 4769394, 4772924, 4772925, 8045038, 8045039, 8045854, 8045855, 8049417, 8389861, 8744901, 9125736, 9126552, 9129116, 9191655, 9195963, 9199526, 11269881, 11269882, 11980920, 12842146, 12842147, 12842148, 12992812, 12994673, 12994674, 13243497, 13243498, 13284319, 13284320, 13287790, 15045897, 17124920, 17155941, 17349716, 17350516, 17834576, 17835376, 17838847, 18709199, 18709200, 19141687, 19145086, 19707761, 19707762, 20395235, 21120528, 21302675, 23029932, 23030717, 23033156, 23543974, 24026977, 24030376, 24267176, 24268112, 24894528, 25124195, 25126569, 25128391, 25907287, 27473160, 27729399, 28069828, 28070647, 28070648, 28074024, 28114008, 30169624, 30169625, 30172937, 30714787, 31384365, 32861553, 34743165, 34812327, 35486209, 35488589, 36119007, 36180825, 36181587, 38559078, 38562283, 38563068, 38565313, 38567058, 38569303, 38570088, 38573293, 38574078, 38577283, 38578068, 38580313, 38581098, 38584303, 38585088, 38588293, 38589078, 38591323, 38593068, 38595313, 38596098, 38599303, 38600088, 38603293, 38604078,

38606323, 38620141, 38620881, 38897305, 38899050, 42094511, 42465442, 43183880, 43184665, 43260160, 43394835, 43398070, 43398810, 43402046, 43402786, 43750978, 44800409, 44800410, 44800411, 44973682, 44974467, 45356362, 45357102, 46257820, 47165564, 47321156, 47321157, 47323327, 47323328, 47494761, 47495478, 47726421, 48341780, 48734094, 48734095, 50134562, 51585137, 51867698, 52360449, 52648662, 53528122, 54213909, 54264295, 54266407, 54267140, 54270148, 54270880, 54270881, 54430365, 54782902, 54783599, 55209653, 55209654, 55349728, 56318241, 56318242, 56318939, 57243691, 57244423, 57244424, 57244425, 57761985, 57849957, 57851508, 57868205, 58164568, 58504322, 58620884, 58620885, 58952200, 58952898, 58955929, 58955930, 58956627, 58958805, 59197526, 59197527, 60436819, 60437552, 61409236, 61409969, 61412977, 61413709, 61416717, 63727308, 63727309, 63738793, 63739500, 63920170, 64076240, 64329170, 64329171, 64593949, 64593950, 66748349, 66920640, 67531748, 68006944, 68087366, 68101930, 68102636, 68105536, 68385185, 68385186, 68385892, 69948427, 69948428, 69949099, 69949100, 71112921, 71112922, 71115741, 71116391, 71653802, 72546138, 72546819, 73235739, 73826238, 73826239, 74203813, 74203814, 74204463, 74207283, 74295784, 74297808, 74299253, 74301277, 74445185, 74448004, 74448005, 74448654, 74448655, 74450678, 74450679, 74452124, 74454148, 74454798, 74457617, 74457618, 74713761, 74870301, 77873655, 79804018, 81355285, 83602337, 83724839, 83727555, 83728183, 85378553, 85668102, 85668103, 85670698, 86204756, 86204757, 86205384, 86205385, 86246103, 86247969, 86714200, 86714201, 86714828, 86714829, 87223888, 87223889, 87225694, 87225695, 87266653, 87266654, 87573245, 88893525, 89003121, 89640885, 90666380, 90666381, 91745469, 92792331, 92792332, 93141136, 93142907, 93143472, 93145934, 93145935, 93146499, 93146500, 93726751, 94384947, 94384948, 94386718, 96059934, 97632231, 97788697, 98668702, 98668703, 98668704, 101185055, 101543106, 101543107, 102185876, 102185877, 102186413, 102906956, 103050553, 103051745, 103053424, 103053425, 103053426, 103053961, 103056296, 103056833, 103682376, 103781915, 103783171, 103783172, 103784796, 103784797, 103836527, 103836528, 104514100, 104514101, 104516436, 104516972, 104985790, 105053945, 105122201, 105561193, 105561194, 106184000, 106844041, 107791465, 107791466, 108072205, 108074371, 108074898, 108077063, 108077590, 108077591, 108077592, 108127698, 108129864, 109183361, 110705590, 110706117, 110708283, 110708810, 110710975, 110710976, 110779861, 110780363, 111232403, 111234431, 111812565, 111812566, 111812567, 111813990, 111813991, 112514199, 113839689, 113839690, 114291183, 114291654, 114293697, 114776038, 114776531, 114777956, 115004584, 115005077, 115007105, 115379975, 115722901, 115723372, 115903726, 115930248, 115930719, 118133584, 118309687, 118311574, 119469050, 119469504, 119471378, 119471379, 119717829

Log Highlights:	====== Destination drive setup ====== 125045424 sectors wiped with 79 ====== Comparison of original to clone drive ====== Sectors compared: 120103200 Sectors match: 120082400 Sectors differ: 20800 Bytes differ: 10628800

```
Diffs range 67392-67455, 68160-68223, 688128-688191,
1768960-1769023, 1772544-1772607, 2215168-2215231,
2664128-2664191, 3155328-3155391, 4768512-4768575,
4769344-4769407, 4772864-4772927, 8044992-8045055,
8045824-8045887, 8049408-8049471, 8389824-8389887,
8744896-8744959, 9125696-9125759, 9126528-9126591,
9129088-9129151, 9191616-9191679, 9195904-9195967,
9199488-9199551, 11269824-11269887, 11980864-11980927,
12842112-12842175, 12992768-12992831, 12994624-12994687,
13243456-13243519, 13284288-13284351, 13287744-13287807,
15045888-15045951, 17124864-17124927, 17155904-17155967,
17349696-17349759, 17350464-17350527, 17834560-17834623,
17835328-17835391, 17838784-17838847, 18709184-18709247,
19141632-19141695, 19145024-19145087, 19707712-19707775,
20395200-20395263, 21120512-21120575, 21302656-21302719,
23029888-23029951, 23030656-23030719, 23033152-23033215,
23543936-23543999, 24026944-24027007, 24030336-24030399,
24267136-24267199, 24268096-24268159, 24894528-24894591,
25124160-25124223, 25126528-25126591, 25128384-25128447,
25907264-25907327, 27473152-27473215, 27729344-27729407,
28069824-28069887, 28070592-28070655, 28073984-28074047,
28113984-28114047, 30169600-30169663, 30172928-30172991,
30714752-30714815, 31384320-31384383, 32861504-32861567,
34743104-34743167, 34812288-34812351, 35486208-35486271,
35488576-35488639, 36118976-36119039, 36180800-36180863,
36181568-36181631, 38559040-38559103, 38562240-38562303,
38563008-38563071, 38565312-38565375, 38567040-38567103,
38569280-38569343, 38570048-38570111, 38573248-38573311,
38574016-38574079, 38577280-38577343, 38578048-38578111,
38580288-38580351, 38581056-38581119, 38584256-38584319,
38585088-38585151, 38588288-38588351, 38589056-38589119,
38591296-38591359, 38593024-38593087, 38595264-38595327,
38596096-38596159, 38599296-38599359, 38600064-38600127,
38603264-38603327, 38604032-38604095, 38606272-38606335,
38620096-38620159, 38620864-38620927, 38897280-38897343,
38899008-38899071, 42094464-42094527, 42465408-42465471,
43183872-43183935, 43184640-43184703, 43260160-43260223,
43394816-43394879, 43398016-43398079, 43398784-43398847,
43401984-43402047, 43402752-43402815, 43750976-43751039,
44800384-44800447, 44973632-44973695, 44974464-44974527,
45356352-45356415, 45357056-45357119, 46257792-46257855,
47165504-47165567, 47321152-47321215, 47323264-47323391,
47494720-47494783, 47495424-47495487, 47726400-47726463,
48341760-48341823, 48734080-48734143, 50134528-50134591,
51585088-51585151, 51867648-51867711, 52360448-52360511,
52648640-52648703, 53528064-53528127, 54213888-54213951,
54264256-54264319, 54266368-54266431, 54267136-54267199,
54270144-54270207, 54270848-54270911, 54430336-54430399,
54782848-54782911, 54783552-54783615, 55209600-55209663,
55349696-55349759, 56318208-56318271, 56318912-56318975,
57243648-57243711, 57244416-57244479, 57761984-57762047,
57849920-57849983, 57851456-57851519, 57868160-57868223,
58164544-58164607, 58504320-58504383, 58620864-58620927,
58952192-58952255, 58952896-58952959, 58955904-58955967,
58956608-58956671, 58958784-58958847, 59197504-59197567,
60436800-60436863, 60437504-60437567, 61409216-61409279,
61409920-61409983, 61412928-61412991, 61413696-61413759,
61416704-61416767, 63727296-63727359, 63738752-63738815,
63739456-63739519, 63920128-63920191, 64076224-64076287,
64329152-64329215, 64593920-64593983, 66748288-66748351,
66920640-66920703, 67531712-67531775, 68006912-68006975,
68087360-68087423, 68101888-68101951, 68102592-68102655,
68105536-68105599, 68385152-68385215, 68385856-68385919,
69948416-69948479, 69949056-69949119, 71112896-71112959,
71115712-71115775, 71116352-71116415, 71653760-71653823,
72546112-72546175, 72546816-72546879, 73235712-73235775,
73826176-73826239, 74203776-74203839, 74204416-74204479,
74207232-74207295, 74295744-74295807, 74297792-74297855,
74299200-74299263, 74301248-74301311, 74445184-74445247,
74448000-74448063, 74448640-74448703, 74450624-74450687,
```

```
74452096-74452159, 74454144-74454207, 74454784-74454847,
74457600-74457663, 74713728-74713791, 74870272-74870335,
77873600-77873663, 79803968-79804031, 81355264-81355327,
83602304-83602367, 83724800-83724863, 83727552-83727615,
83728128-83728191, 85378496-85378559, 85668096-85668159,
85670656-85670719, 86204736-86204799, 86205376-86205439,
86246080-86246143, 86247936-86247999, 86714176-86714239,
86714816-86714879, 87223872-87223935, 87225664-87225727,
87266624-87266687, 87573184-87573247, 88893504-88893567,
89003072-89003135, 89640832-89640895, 90666368-90666431,
91745408-91745471, 92792320-92792383, 93141120-93141183,
93142848-93142911, 93143424-93143487, 93145920-93145983,
93146496-93146559, 93726720-93726783, 94384896-94384959,
94386688-94386751, 96059904-96059967, 97632192-97632255,
97788672-97788735, 98668672-98668735, 101185024-101185087,
101543104-101543167, 102185856-102185919, 102186368-102186431,
102906944-102907007, 103050496-103050559, 103051712-103051775,
103053376-103053439, 103053952-103054015, 103056256-103056319,
103056832-103056895, 103682368-103682431, 103781888-103781951,
103783168-103783231, 103784768-103784831, 103836480-103836543,
104514048-104514111, 104516416-104516479, 104516928-104516991,
104985728-104985791, 105053888-105053951, 105122176-105122239,
105561152-105561215, 106184000-106184063, 106844032-106844095,
107791424-107791487, 108072192-108072255, 108074368-108074431,
108074880-108074943, 108077056-108077119, 108077568-108077631,
108127680-108127743, 108129856-108129919, 109183360-109183423,
110705536-110705599, 110706112-110706175, 110708224-110708287,
110708800-110708863, 110710912-110711039, 110779840-110779903,
110780352-110780415, 111232384-111232447, 111234368-111234431,
111812544-111812607, 111813952-111814015, 112514176-112514239,
113839680-113839743, 114291136-114291199, 114291648-114291711,
114293696-114293759, 114776000-114776063, 114776512-114776575,
114777920-114777983, 115004544-115004607, 115005056-115005119,
115007104-115007167, 115379968-115380031, 115722880-115722943,
115723328-115723391, 115903680-115903743, 115930240-115930303,
115930688-115930751, 118133568-118133631, 118309632-118309695,
118311552-118311615, 119468992-119469055, 119469504-119469567,
119471360-119471423, 119717824-119717887
Source (120103200) has 4942224 fewer sectors than destination (125045424)
Zero fill:                  0
Src Byte fill (ED):         0
Dst Byte fill (79):   4942224
Other fill:                 0
Other no fill:              0
Zero fill range:
Src fill range:
Dst fill range:   120103200-125045423
Other fill range:
Other not filled range:
0 source read errors, 0 destination read errors


====== Tool Settings ======
error-recovery fast


======== Excerpt from Log file ========
Task: Disk to Disk
Case:   DA-09_FAST
# of sectors acquired: 120,103,200 (61.4 GB)
Total errors: 325
Errors recorded: 127
<<WARNING: ERROR LIST TRUNCATED>>
------------------List of errors------------------------
Error # 1: Read error (source), address=67392, length=64
Error # 2: Read error (source), address=68160, length=64
Error # 3: Read error (source), address=688128, length=64
Error # 4: Read error (source), address=1768960, length=64
    . . .
Error # 124: Read error (source), address=47165504, length=64
```

Test Case DA-09-FAST Tableau TD1 Version 2.34	
	Error # 125: Read error (source), address=47321152, length=64 Error # 126: Read error (source), address=47323264, length=64 Error # 127: Read error (source), address=47323328, length=64 <<WARNING: ERROR LIST TRUNCATED>> ======== End of Excerpt from Log file ========
Results:	

Assertion & Expected Result	Actual Result
AM-01 Source acquired using interface AI.	as expected
AM-02 Source is type DS.	as expected
AM-03 Execution environment is XE.	as expected
AM-05 An image is created on file system type FS.	as expected
AM-06 All visible sectors acquired.	some sectors skipped
AM-08 All sectors accurately acquired.	as expected
AM-09 Error logged.	as expected
AM-10 Benign fill replaces inaccessible sectors.	as expected
AO-01 Image file is complete and accurate.	as expected
AO-05 Multifile image created.	as expected
AO-22 Tool calculates hashes by block.	option not available
AO-23 Logged information is correct.	as expected
AO-24 Source is unchanged by acquisition.	not checked

Analysis:	Expected results not achieved

5.2.19 DA-10-E01

Test Case DA-10-E01 Tableau TD1 Version 2.34	
Case Summary:	DA-10 Acquire a digital source to an image file in an alternate format.
Assertions:	AM-01 The tool uses access interface SRC-AI to access the digital source. AM-02 The tool acquires digital source DS. AM-03 The tool executes in execution environment XE. AM-05 If image file creation is specified, the tool creates an image file on file system type FS. AM-06 All visible sectors are acquired from the digital source. AM-08 All sectors acquired from the digital source are acquired accurately. AO-01 If the tool creates an image file, the data represented by the image file is the same as the data acquired by the tool. AO-02 If an image file format is specified, the tool creates an image file in the specified format. AO-05 If the tool creates a multi-file image of a requested size then all the individual files shall be no larger than the requested size. AO-22 If requested, the tool calculates block hashes for a specified block size during an acquisition for each block acquired from the digital source. AO-23 If the tool logs any log significant information, the information is accurately recorded in the log file. AO-24 If the tool executes in a forensically safe execution environment, the digital source is unchanged by the acquisition process.
Tester Name:	brl
Test Host:	TD1
Test Date:	Wed Mar 23 13:29:29 2011
Drives:	src(43) dst (none) other (64-SATA)
Source Setup:	src hash (SHA256): < 2658F47603DE6B1D883B64823E9733F578658D08D06A4BB8C053C4F57BDC615E > src hash (SHA1): < 888E2E7F7AD237DC7A732281DD93F325065E5871 > src hash (MD5): < BC39C3F7EE7A50E77B9BA1E65A5AEEF7 > 78125000 total sectors (40000000000 bytes) Model (0BB-75JHC0) serial # (WD-WMAMC46588) <pre> N Start LBA Length Start C/H/S End C/H/S boot Partition type 1 P 000000063 020980827 0000/001/01 1023/254/63 0C Fat32X 2 X 020980890 057143205 1023/000/01 1023/254/63 0F extended 3 S 000000063 000032067 1023/001/01 1023/254/63 01 Fat12 4 x 000032130 002104515 1023/000/01 1023/254/63 05 extended 5 S 000000063 002104452 1023/001/01 1023/254/63 06 Fat16 6 x 002136645 004192965 1023/000/01 1023/254/63 05 extended 7 S 000000063 004192902 1023/001/01 1023/254/63 16 other 8 x 006329610 008401995 1023/000/01 1023/254/63 05 extended 9 S 000000063 008401932 1023/001/01 1023/254/63 0B Fat32 10 x 014731605 010490445 1023/000/01 1023/254/63 05 extended 11 S 000000063 010490382 1023/001/01 1023/254/63 83 Linux 12 x 025222050 004209030 1023/000/01 1023/254/63 05 extended 13 S 000000063 004208967 1023/001/01 1023/254/63 82 Linux swap 14 x 029431080 027712125 1023/000/01 1023/254/63 05 extended 15 S 000000063 027712062 1023/001/01 1023/254/63 07 NTFS 16 S 000000000 000000000 0000/000/00 0000/000/00 00 empty entry 17 P 000000000 000000000 0000/000/00 0000/000/00 00 empty entry 18 P 000000000 000000000 0000/000/00 0000/000/00 00 empty entry 1 020980827 sectors 10742183424 bytes 3 000032067 sectors 16418304 bytes 5 002104452 sectors 1077479424 bytes 7 004192902 sectors 2146765824 bytes 9 008401932 sectors 4301789184 bytes 11 010490382 sectors 5371075584 bytes 13 004208967 sectors 2154991104 bytes 15 027712062 sectors 14188575744 bytes</pre>
Log Highlights:	====== Tool Settings ====== verify-hash off

```
====== Image file segments ======
     1       2136 2011-03-23 13:52 2011-03-23 13-36-23 00009 D2F.LOG
     2 2081549778 2011-03-23 13:36 IMAGE.E01
     3  217575011 2011-03-23 13:50 IMAGE.E02

======== Excerpt from Log file ========
Task: Disk to File
Case:  DA-10-E01
# of sectors acquired: 78,125,000 (40.0 GB)
Chunk size in sectors: 4,194,304 (2.1 GB)
Chunks expected: 19
Chunks written: 2
Source hash:
 SHA1: 888e2e7f7ad237dc7a732281dd93f325065e5871
 MD5 : bc39c3f7ee7a50e77b9ba1e65a5aeef7

======== End of Excerpt from Log file ========

====== Source drive rehash ======
Rehash (SHA1) of source: 888E2E7F7AD237DC7A732281DD93F325065E5871
```

Results:

Assertion & Expected Result	Actual Result
AM-01 Source acquired using interface AI.	as expected
AM-02 Source is type DS.	as expected
AM-03 Execution environment is XE.	as expected
AM-05 An image is created on file system type FS.	as expected
AM-06 All visible sectors acquired.	as expected
AM-08 All sectors accurately acquired.	as expected
AO-01 Image file is complete and accurate.	as expected
AO-02 Image file in specified format.	as expected
AO-05 Multifile image created.	as expected
AO-22 Tool calculates hashes by block.	option not available
AO-23 Logged information is correct.	as expected
AO-24 Source is unchanged by acquisition.	as expected

Analysis: Expected results achieved

5.2.20   DA-13

Test Case DA-13 Tableau TD1 Version 2.34	
Case Summary:	DA-13 Create an image file where there is insufficient space on a single volume, and use destination device switching to continue on another volume.
Assertions:	AM-01 The tool uses access interface SRC-AI to access the digital source.
	AM-02 The tool acquires digital source DS.
	AM-03 The tool executes in execution environment XE.
	AM-05 If image file creation is specified, the tool creates an image file on file system type FS.
	AM-06 All visible sectors are acquired from the digital source.
	AM-08 All sectors acquired from the digital source are acquired accurately.
	AO-01 If the tool creates an image file, the data represented by the image file is the same as the data acquired by the tool.
	AO-04 If the tool is creating an image file and there is insufficient space on the image destination device to contain the image file, the tool shall notify the user.
	AO-05 If the tool creates a multi-file image of a requested size then all the individual files shall be no larger than the requested size.
	AO-10 If there is insufficient space to contain all files of a multi-file image and if destination device switching is supported, the image is continued on another device.
	AO-22 If requested, the tool calculates block hashes for a specified block size during an acquisition for each block acquired from the digital source.
	AO-23 If the tool logs any log significant information, the information is accurately recorded in the log file.
	AO-24 If the tool executes in a forensically safe execution environment, the digital source is unchanged by the acquisition process.
Tester Name:	brl
Test Host:	TD1
Test Date:	Wed Mar 23 10:06:05 2011
Drives:	src(41) dst (39-SATA) other (90)
Source Setup:	src hash (SHA256): < FBF3AA21489653D880FFAE71449A9F7E8EE4F56A6C3BF58A3A3FFB13203F1B1D >
	src hash (SHA1): < 15CAA1A307271160D8372668BF8A03FC45A51CC9 >
	src hash (MD5): < 0A6A8EF78BDC14E2026710D8CCB5607C >
	78125000 total sectors (40000000000 bytes)
	65534/015/63 (max cyl/hd values)
	65535/016/63 (number of cyl/hd)
	IDE disk: Model (WDC WD400BB-75JHC0) serial # (WD-WMAMC4658355)
	N Start LBA Length Start C/H/S End C/H/S boot Partition type
	1 P 000000063 078107967 0000/001/01 1023/254/63 Boot 07 NTFS
	2 P 000000000 000000000 0000/000/00 0000/000/00 00 empty entry
	3 P 000000000 000000000 0000/000/00 0000/000/00 00 empty entry
	4 P 000000000 000000000 0000/000/00 0000/000/00 00 empty entry
	1 078107967 sectors 39991279104 bytes
Log Highlights:	====== Tool Settings ======
	verify-hash off
	====== Image file segments (First destination) ======
	1 -rwx------ 1 ubuntu root 3999989760 2011-03-23 13:16 IMAGE.001
	2 -rwx------ 1 ubuntu root 3999989760 2011-03-23 13:18 IMAGE.002
	3 -rwx------ 1 ubuntu root 3999989760 2011-03-23 13:20 IMAGE.003
	. . .
	5 -rwx------ 1 ubuntu root 3999989760 2011-03-23 13:24 IMAGE.005
	6 -rwx------ 1 ubuntu root 3999989760 2011-03-23 13:27 IMAGE.006
	7 -rwx------ 1 ubuntu root 3999989760 2011-03-23 13:29 IMAGE.007
	====== Image file segments (Final destination) ======
	1 2643 2011-03-23 13:43 2011-03-23 13-15-58 00012 D2F.LOG
	2 3999989760 2011-03-23 13:37 IMAGE.008
	3 3999989760 2011-03-23 13:39 IMAGE.009
	4 3999989760 2011-03-23 13:41 IMAGE.010
	5 102400 2011-03-23 13:42 IMAGE.011

```
Test Case DA-13 Tableau TD1 Version 2.34
```

```
======== Excerpt from Log file ========
Task: Disk to File
Case:   DA-13
# of sectors acquired: 78,125,000 (40.0 GB)
Chunk size in sectors: 7,812,480 (3.9 GB)
Chunks expected: 11
Chunks written: 11
Source hash:
 SHA1: 15caa1a307271160d8372668bf8a03fc45a51cc9
 MD5 : 0a6a8ef78bdc14e2026710d8ccb5607c

======== End of Excerpt from Log file ========

====== Source drive rehash ======
Rehash (SHA1) of source: 15CAA1A307271160D8372668BF8A03FC45A51CC9
```

Results:

Assertion & Expected Result	Actual Result
AM-01 Source acquired using interface AI.	as expected
AM-02 Source is type DS.	as expected
AM-03 Execution environment is XE.	as expected
AM-05 An image is created on file system type FS.	as expected
AM-06 All visible sectors acquired.	as expected
AM-08 All sectors accurately acquired.	as expected
AO-01 Image file is complete and accurate.	as expected
AO-04 User notified if space exhausted.	as expected
AO-05 Multifile image created.	as expected
AO-10 Image file continued on new device.	as expected
AO-22 Tool calculates hashes by block.	option not available
AO-23 Logged information is correct.	as expected
AO-24 Source is unchanged by acquisition.	as expected

Analysis: Expected results achieved

About the National Institute of Justice

A component of the Office of Justice Programs, NIJ is the research, development and evaluation agency of the U.S. Department of Justice. NIJ's mission is to advance scientific research, development and evaluation to enhance the administration of justice and public safety. NIJ's principal authorities are derived from the Omnibus Crime Control and Safe Streets Act of 1968, as amended (see 42 U.S.C. §§ 3721–3723).

The NIJ Director is appointed by the President and confirmed by the Senate. The Director establishes the Institute's objectives, guided by the priorities of the Office of Justice Programs, the U.S. Department of Justice, and the needs of the field. The Institute actively solicits the views of criminal justice and other professionals and researchers to inform its search for the knowledge and tools to guide policy and practice.

Strategic Goals

NIJ has seven strategic goals grouped into three categories:

Creating relevant knowledge and tools

1. Partner with state and local practitioners and policymakers to identify social science research and technology needs.
2. Create scientific, relevant, and reliable knowledge—with a particular emphasis on terrorism, violent crime, drugs and crime, cost-effectiveness, and community-based efforts—to enhance the administration of justice and public safety.
3. Develop affordable and effective tools and technologies to enhance the administration of justice and public safety.

Dissemination

4. Disseminate relevant knowledge and information to practitioners and policymakers in an understandable, timely and concise manner.
5. Act as an honest broker to identify the information, tools and technologies that respond to the needs of stakeholders.

Agency management

6. Practice fairness and openness in the research and development process.
7. Ensure professionalism, excellence, accountability, cost-effectiveness and integrity in the management and conduct of NIJ activities and programs.

Program Areas

In addressing these strategic challenges, the Institute is involved in the following program areas: crime control and prevention, including policing; drugs and crime; justice systems and offender behavior, including corrections; violence and victimization; communications and information technologies; critical incident response; investigative and forensic sciences, including DNA; less-than-lethal technologies; officer protection; education and training technologies; testing and standards; technology assistance to law enforcement and corrections agencies; field testing of promising programs; and international crime control.

In addition to sponsoring research and development and technology assistance, NIJ evaluates programs, policies, and technologies. NIJ communicates its research and evaluation findings through conferences and print and electronic media.

To find out more about the National Institute of Justice, please visit:

www.nij.gov

or contact:

National Criminal Justice
  Reference Service
P.O. Box 6000
Rockville, MD 20849–6000
800–851–3420
http://www.ncjrs.gov